MANMADE WONDERS

Patricia Sechi-Johnson

DRAGON'S WORLD

CHILDREN'S BOOKS

DRAGON'S WORLD

CHILDREN'S BOOKS

Dragon's World Ltd
Limpsfield
Surrey RH8 0DY
Great Britain

First published by Dragon's World Ltd, 1996

© Dragon's World Ltd, 1996

British Library
Cataloguing in Publication Data
The catalogue record for this book is
available from the British Library.

ISBN 1 85028 314 1

Editor: Diana Briscoe
Picture researcher: Richard Philpott
Designer: Mel Raymond
Art Director: John Strange
Design Assistants: Karen Ferguson
                    Victoria Furbisher
DTP Manager: Michael Burgess
Editorial Director: Pippa Rubinstein

Typeset by Dragon's World Ltd
in Stempel Garamond and Gill

Printed in Italy

Contents

Introduction

The natural world has some awesome sites such as the Grand Canyon, Niagara Falls and the Himalayas, but man has created wonders to rival them. Perhaps they are even more amazing because they have been achieved by the skill and hard work of human beings.

Over the centuries we have changed the shape of the landscape, built the most monumentally large structures, dug tunnels in the earth and dragged huge stones miles and miles to create massive buildings. Even today with the aid of modern machinery it is hard to imagine man being capable of such feats.

We are still overwhelmed by the scale of many ancient sites which man created but, the modern ones too, leave us speechless. We have created machines capable of sending men into space, stopped the seas by constructing dams, built high into the sky and created some stunningly beautiful buildings and bridges.

This book aims to gather together 100 of the most tantalizing and spectacular

manmade wonders in a mixture of statues, gardens, religious buildings, carvings, telescopes, industrial structures, even whole cities! Perhaps reading through you may find that some of the structures have been created in the same way, some were forgotten for centuries until modern times and others have always been thought amazing manmade wonders.

Patricia Sechi-Johnson

OPPOSITE
TOP LEFT: Stonehenge, England.
TOP RIGHT: Geodesic dome, Montreal, Canada.
BOTTOM: Machu Picchu, Peru.

RIGHT: the *Troll* gas-drilling platform.
BELOW: the Taj Mahal, India.

The Seven Wonders of the World

The Seven Wonders of the World were buildings and statues from the ancient world which were amazing for their size, beauty, or the way they were built. The two not shown here were the Pyramids of Egypt and the Temple of Artemis at Ephesus. The list was compiled some time in the third century BC. By today's standards, we may feel that they are not particularly remarkable for their size. However, they would still be admired for their beauty and age.

The Temple of Artemis was built by King Croesus of Lydia in Ephesus, Turkey, to Artemis, goddess of birth and fertility. It burnt down in 356 BC. Of the Seven Wonders, only the pyramids of Giza (see page 11) remain. Pieces of the Mausoleum and the Temple of Artemis can be seen in the British Museum in London.

▲ The Mausoleum, or tomb of Mausolus, of Halicarnassus was said to be about 40 m high. Columns stood at the base with a stepped pyramid on top. A statue of Mausolus, the King of Caria, probably stood at the summit. It was destroyed by an earthquake in the third century AD.

◄ The Colossus was built at the entrance to the harbour of the town of Rhodes. It was a statue of Helios, the Greek sun-god and stood about 33 m high. It was destroyed by an earthquake in 226 BC, about fifty years after it was finished.

▼ The Pharos, or Lighthouse, of Alexandria was built on an artificial island on the orders of Alexander the Great in about 300 BC. It was at least 122 m high and made of gleaming white limestone or marble.

▲ The statue of Zeus at Olympus was the creation of the Greek sculptor Phidias. He made Zeus's flesh out of ivory and his robe out of gold.

▼ Writers who saw the Hanging Gardens of Babylon described a terraced structure which had tiers planted with palms, and other trees. The gardens were built by Nebuchadnezzar in about 570 BC.

Step Pyramid, Egypt

King Zoser ruled ancient Egypt around 2650 to 2575 BC. He became famous for the technological advances made during his reign. When Zoser decided to have a tomb built he asked his architect and chancellor, Imhotep, to design one for him. Imhotep came up with a pyramid. This was a revolutionary new shape for a tomb as up until then tombs had been flat-topped rectangular structures.

Zoser's pyramid was built at Saqqara, near the old capital of Memphis. It is called the Step Pyramid because it rises up in six stages. The pyramid was constructed entirely out of stone which was a new idea, too. Egyptian tombs had always been built of mud bricks. The Step Pyramid is the earliest stone building in Egypt. Inside passageways over 30 m deep led to the royal burial chambers.

▲ Pyramid decoration had reached a high standard at Saqqara as can be seen in this wall carving in the tomb of Ptah Hotep.

▼ The pyramid of Zoser stood in a huge funeral complex which was surrounded by a wall. The site also enclosed a number of white stone temples.

Several other Egyptian pharaohs also built pyramids at Saqqara. One of the pharaohs, called Unas, was the first to have writing on the walls of the burial chambers inside his pyramid. These writings are called Pyramid Texts. They were intended to protect the pharaoh and ensure him life after death. Later pharaohs continued having Pyramid Texts painted inside their pyramids.

Pyramids at Giza, Egypt

The ten pyramids at Giza in Egypt are one of the Seven Ancient Wonders of the World. They stand near the banks of the River Nile, rising out of the desert. They are so large that it is easy to believe the ancient legends that they were built by gods or giants.

The three largest and best-preserved pyramids were built by three pharaohs – Khufu, Khafre and Menkaure – between 2600 and 2500 BC. The largest is the Great Pyramid of Khufu. It is an almost solid stone mass and contains more than two million stones. The huge blocks were moved by groups of men who dragged them up earth ramps, built as a sort of scaffolding around the pyramid.

The pyramids were built as tombs. The ancient Egyptians believed in life after death and burial chambers inside the pyramids were originally crammed with gold and precious objects.

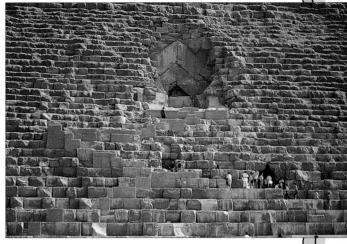

▲ The outer layer of white stones which originally covered the pyramids has almost disappeared and the stone blocks beneath are now visible, exposing its inner structure.

▼ The pyramid of Khufu is the largest of the ten pyramids. In front of the pyramid of Khafre stands a large statue of the Sphinx.

Films about ancient Egypt often show slaves being cruelly whipped as they struggle on the pyramids. Fortunately, this was not how it actually was. Every yea then, the Nile flooded covering the fields for 3–4 months. The farmers and labourers could not work the fields, so they found other work building tombs. It may have taken 30 or so years to complete a pyramid.

Ziggurat, Ur

The ziggurat of Ur towered above this great city which stood near the River Euphrates in the ancient land of Mesopotamia (now modern Iraq). The ziggurat was built by the Sumerian people between 2112 and 2095 BC during the reign of king Ur-Nammu. It was a solid mass of brick and measured 64 x 46 m at the base. Originally the ziggurat stood in the corner of a sacred area which contained other temples.

A ziggurat is a temple tower and it looks very similar to a pyramid. This one had three staircases of a hundred steps each, leading to a gateway between the first and second terraces. From here a further staircase led to the top of the ziggurat and a small shrine to the moon god Nannu, who was the god of the city. Much of the ziggurat remained standing over the centuries making it the most important building left by the Sumerian people.

▲ The huge structure of the ziggurat of Ur towers above the desert of Iraq.

The prophet, Abraham, was born and lived in Ur when the city was surrounded by a moat and stood in the middle of lush farmland. Now Ur lies in a desert area half covered by sand drifts, and the River Euphrates no longer flows past the city. It has been re-routed to run in a different direction.

◀ The ziggurat of Ur had three impressive staircases which led to the second level of the temple.

Grimes Graves, Norfolk

Stone Age humans achieved some remarkable feats of engineering, such as Stonehenge (see page 16) – they also dug mines. In Norfolk, the countryside is marked by hollows which are filled-in Stone Age mines. Flint mining was a large industry here between 2000 and 1800 BC. Flint was one of the best materials for early humans to make tools, and the stone could be traded for goods.

Grimes Graves are the best-known flint mines in Britain. Some of the shafts are 9 m deep with tunnels branching out at the bottom. No supports were used to hold up the tunnels, which meant they could not be dug too deep or too high. Instead, lots of shafts seem to have been dug in one spot. The pits were lit by simple oil lamps. The miners probably climbed up and down ladders to get in and out of the pits.

▼ It has been guessed that it took twenty men about a hundred days to cut out a shaft and another forty to dig out the galleries.

▲ Miners cut away the rock using picks made of deer antlers and flint tools.

Not every region had flint. Stone Age communities living near large quantities of the stone mined it for their own use and traded any that was extra to their needs. Flint was still being worked in Norfolk until this century. The flints were used in flintlock pistols and guns which were sent to the USA and Africa.

Palace of Knossos, Crete

The Minoan civilization was one of the earliest to spring up around the Aegean Sea. Until a hundred years ago, it was only thought to exist in myths. Legend told of a monster called the Minotaur, half-man, half-bull, who lived in a maze called the Labyrinth. The son of Queen Pasiphae, her husband, King Minos, had the maze built to hide away the horrible beast. Every year the Minotaur devoured seven young men and seven young women until a Greek prince, Theseus, killed him.

When the Englishman, Sir Arthur ⌐ found the Palace of Knossos on Crete, he seriou. .ieved it to be the legendary labyrinth. When he b͞ to dig on the site, he realized it was a large palace with more than 1,000 rooms on five floors. Dating from 1700 to1450 BC, it is a rambling building spreading across a hillside. It was built by a sophisticated people who had even created an elaborate drainage system. Many regard the Minoan civilization as the first European civilization.

▲ Bulls featured largely in Minoan beliefs and culture. It is probable that the bull dancing and leaping ceremonies were performed at Knossos. This pair of bull-shaped horns carved in stone stands in the grounds of the palace.

The Palace of Knossos has been a keenly discussed matter ever since it was restored by Arthur Evans. Many historians think that the building he recreated is not how the original would have looked, but came straight out of Evans' imagination. Some of the wall paintings were moved or redrawn, and his view of Cretan history is now doubted.

▼ Several rooms in the palace are painted with scenes of dancing, sports, dolphins and processions. The top-heavy pillars are a particular feature of the palace.

Temples of Abu Simbel, Egypt

The temples of Abu Simbel in Egypt truly deserve to be called great wonders of the world. Not only is it amazing that such huge structures were built without machinery, but also that they have been lost, found and moved. Carved into a rocky mountainside, the two temples stood on the banks of the Nile. They were built by the pharaoh Rameses II, who reigned from 1290 to 1224 BC.

The largest temple stretches 55 m into the mountainside. The nearby smaller temple of Neferari, Rameses' wife, has six standing statues outside. Four are of Rameses and two are of Neferari, each measuring 10 m high. The temples were unknown until 1813 as they were buried in sand. They were dug out in 1817 and have been a tourist attraction ever since.

▲ Inside the temples are elaborately carved with statues and brightly painted walls and ceilings.

Incredibly, these huge temples were moved in 1965–9. They were to be covered by Lake Nasser, formed by the building of the Aswan High Dam. It was a race against time to cut the temples into over a thousand numbered blocks and carefully move them to higher ground. There the blocks were reassembled like a giant jigsaw puzzle, only this time using machines.

▼ The main temple of Abu Simbel is guarded by four 20 m-high statues of the pharaoh Rameses II.

Stonehenge, England

Stonehenge is an ancient monument on Salisbury Plain, in south-western England. It is a group of roughly cut stones set in circles. The stones have been connected with mysteries and strange stories for centuries because no one really knows what Stonehenge was used for. There are many theories about it, some very complicated and wild, but none of them have been proven.

Stonehenge was built in three phases from about 3000 to 1100 BC beginning with a circular ditch and earth bank. The ring of large stones we all think of as Stonehenge was built about 2100 to 2000 BC. A smaller ring of stones stands inside this and two horse-shaped sets of stones inside that.

▲ Stonehenge contains a large ring of stones linked by smaller stones lying across them. Inside stands a smaller stone circle.

▼ Stonehenge could have been used for astronomical purposes – the sun lines up with various stones on certain days of the year.

Stonehenge was built in an area which contained tombs and temples already several hundred years old. Stonehenge itself was a sacred site for many centuries, but we do not know when or why the site was abandoned. Unfortunately, over the centuries, some stones have been carried away for building, while others have fallen down.

A recent and popular idea is that Stonehenge has an astronomical purpose. Stonehenge lines up with the sunrise on the longest day of the year, which could mean that its builders were sun worshippers. It was certainly not built by druids – they did not come into existence until long after Stonehenge was abandoned.

Ishtar Gate, Babylon

In ancient times many cities were surrounded by walls and had to be entered through large gateways, but not many cities had one as stunning as the Ishtar Gate of Babylon. It was one of the eight gateways leading into the city, but it was the only one covered in bright blue bricks and decorated with pictures of dragons, lions and bulls.

The city gateways were all named after gods, and Ishtar was the goddess both of love and war. The Ishtar Gate stood on the Processional Way, which led to the part of Babylon containing temples and palaces. Babylon was one of the wealthiest cities in the ancient world. It lay on the banks of the River Euphrates in Mesopotamia (modern Iraq).

King Nebuchadnezzar II who reigned from 606 to 562 BC rebuilt Babylon on a grand scale and the city became famous for its Hanging Gardens (see page 9) and its huge walls.

▲ Archaeologists who dug at Babylon earlier this century found huge numbers of coloured glazed bricks and were able to piece together the Ishtar Gate. This is a detail of the animals decorating it.

Ishtar was a very important goddess in Babylonian mythology. She was the radiant goddess of love, the Queen of Heaven. Her symbol was Venus, the morning star. However, in another aspect, she was also the Lady of Sorrows and Battles. When she acted as the war goddess, her symbol was a lion.

The strong city walls were wide enough to drive a four-horse chariot around. There was also the great ziggurat (temple tower). This is thought by some historians to be the Tower of Babel, as mentioned in the Bible.

◀ There is little to be seen at Babylon today. However, this may be how the Ishtar Gate would have looked when first built.

The Tunnel of Samos

The Samos Tunnel is a little-known work of ancient Greek engineering. Perhaps because it was built underground, it was forgotten until the nineteenth century when it was rediscovered.

The tunnel was built around 525 BC on the Greek island of Samos. It is 2 m across and travels 100 m through a mountain. The ruler of Samos, Polycrates, ordered that the tunnel be built – it was to carry water to his capital from the other side of the mountain. There were no wells inside the walls of Polycrates's city, and he realized that if his city was attacked, he would be forced to surrender.

Eupalinus was the engineer responsible for the idea of the tunnel. Tunnelling began from both ends. Eupalinus may have placed a line of poles over the mountain to decide where digging should start on each side. All went well until the diggers were near each other and it was discovered that the two ends would not meet. But they were very close and the tunnels were easily joined.

▲ The Samos Tunnel was carved out of a limestone mountain by teams of slaves using pickaxes, hammers and chisels.

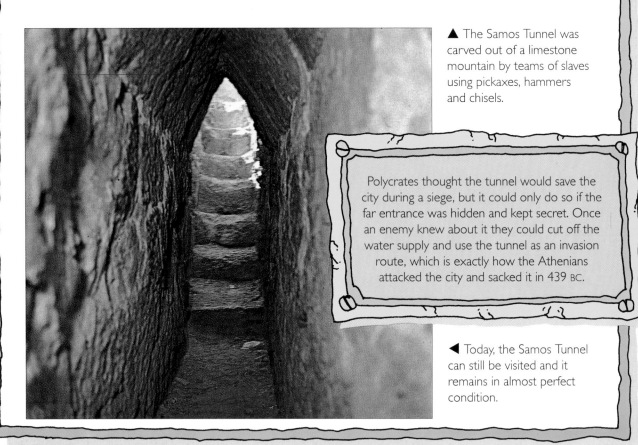

Polycrates thought the tunnel would save the city during a siege, but it could only do so if the far entrance was hidden and kept secret. Once an enemy knew about it they could cut off the water supply and use the tunnel as an invasion route, which is exactly how the Athenians attacked the city and sacked it in 439 BC.

◀ Today, the Samos Tunnel can still be visited and it remains in almost perfect condition.

Great Serpent Mound, Ohio

When settlers in North America first began to travel west, they found strange mounds of earth in the mid-west and southern USA. Some of the raised mounds formed animal shapes, others were more cone-shaped or like flat-topped pyramids.

The different mounds were built by three native peoples who lived in early North America, the Adena, the Hopewell and the Mississippian people. The Adena built animal-shaped mounds, such as Great Serpent Mound, Ohio, around 1000–300 BC. It is the most striking of the many animal mounds. It was not used for burials, but for religious purposes.

Around 300 BC, the Hopewell started building burial mounds surrounded by

▲ A section of the Great Serpent Mound, revealing its sinuous curves – just like a real snake gliding across the plain.

For many years, people did not believe that native Americans had built the mounds until it was proven by excavations in 1881–8. This century, the writings of a sixteenth-century Spanish explorer were discovered in which he recorded having seen Native Americans building mounds in what is the south-east USA.

walls. The Hopewell buried their dead with large quantities of gifts, such as jewellery and pottery. The last group of mound builders, the Mississippian people, built pyramid-shaped mounds from the ninth to the sixteenth century. They buried their dead with even more elaborate gifts.

◀ The earth mound at Great Serpent Mound seems to be formed in the shape of a snake swallowing an egg.

Temple of Neptune, Paestum

The ancient site of Paestum in Italy spreads over a large area. The city was a Greek colony founded in the sixth century BC. Later, in 273 BC, it was settled by the Romans, but abandoned in the ninth century AD. Today, Paestum is a desolate place with many unrecognizable ruins.

In the midst of these ruins are three of the best-preserved Greek temples glowing in golden stone. The Temple of Neptune, built around 450 BC, is the most complete with only the roof and inner walls missing. The other temples on the site are the Temple of Ceres and the larger Basilica of Hera (or Juno), which was built about a century earlier.

The Temple of Neptune is a clever design because its width is half its length and its height is half its width. The temple has an inner room where a large statue of Neptune probably stood.

▲ The huge pillars of the temple of Neptune have survived almost intact over the centuries.

Paestum had been called Poseidonia by the Greeks after the sea god Poseidon whom the Romans called Neptune. The city was renamed by the Romans, who later settled there and enlarged the town adding an amphitheatre, a town hall and a market centre.

▼ A temple was the house of the god for the ancient Greeks and the centre of religious rituals.

The Acropolis, Athens

You may think that the only acropolis is found in Athens, but did you know that they were built all over ancient Greece? An acropolis was the Greek name for any religious and military site built on a hilltop in or near a city.

The Acropolis in Athens is on a rocky hill above the city. After a Persian attack in 480 BC, when many of the buildings in Athens were demolished, the Athenians built a magnificent new group of temples on the Acropolis.

The Parthenon is the largest temple on the Acropolis, and it was built in honour of Athena, the patron goddess of the city. It is probably the best and most famous of all ancient Greek temples. It was constructed between 447 and 432 BC using only white marble. All around the outside, brightly painted sculptures decorated the temple pediment (the band above the pillars).

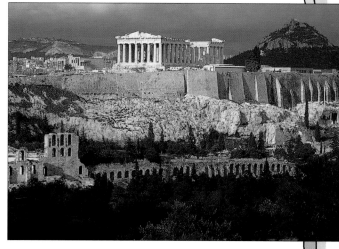

▲ The Acropolis in Athens stands on the highest hilltop and dominates the city.

The Parthenon has had many uses in its history. About AD 500, it became a Christian church. In the fifteenth century, the Turks captured the city and the Parthenon was turned into a mosque. Later, in 1687, it was used to store gunpowder, and during an attack by the Venetians the Parthenon was blown up.

▼ Caryatids, or statues of women, hold up the porch of the Erechtheum.

The Erechtheum is a smaller temple on the Acropolis built from 421 to 406 BC. It, too, is famous. Its porch is held up by six columns carved in the shape of women. The ruins of many other temples and shrines remain on the hilltop. They were once all surrounded by a wall and reached through an entrance hall called the Propylaea.

The Theatre, Epidaurus

Going to see a play for the ancient Greeks would have been just as exciting as it is for us today, although perhaps not as comfortable. The seats in a Greek theatre were all cut out of stone and resembled giant steps.

The theatre at Epidaurus is probably the best-preserved example of a Greek theatre. It is a semi-circle and, like many Greek theatres, it was built into a hillside in about 450 BC. It formed part of the Temple of Asklepios, Greek god of healing.

The seats are arranged into wedge-shaped sections divided by stairs to get in and out of the rows. These slope down steeply to a round area called the orchestra, which is where the actors would have performed.

Behind them stood a long building, which Epidaurus no longer has. It was called the scene and it provided permanent scenery and the actors' changing rooms.

▲ The theatre at Epidaurus was vast and could hold over 12,000 people. Today, it is still in use for summer festivals and performances.

The sound in a Greek theatre was very important, especially as no electrical means of amplifying sound were known. At Epidaurus the acoustics was so good that an actor whispering in the orchestra area could be heard on the very top row of seats.

Great Wall, China

The Great Wall of China is the largest manmade construction in the world. It is so huge that it can even be seen from space. The first sections of wall were probably begun as early as 400 BC.

However, it was the Emperor Shi Huangdi, who ruled from 221 to 210 BC, who planned the Great Wall. He decided to erect new walls to connect the lengths of wall already built. Work continued on the wall until AD 618. Eventually, much of it fell down and was rebuilt between 1368 and 1644.

The Great Wall protected China from small attacks, but it could not stop a major invasion. In the thirteenth century, the mighty leader, Genghis Khan, swept across the Wall with his Mongol armies and invaded much of China.

There are actually two walls about 7.6 m high which run side by side. The area in the middle has been filled with earth and paved over with bricks. The wall is nearly 2,900 km long. Watchtowers, from where guards could raise the alarm, are dotted along its length.

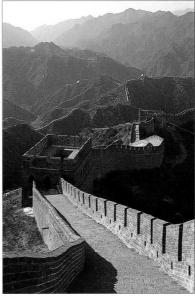

▲ The watchtowers along the wall once served as customs posts.

▼ The Great Wall of China follows a winding course stretching over hills, mountains and deserts.

The Emperor Shi Huangdi was the first man to rule over all China. When he died, he was buried along with a life-size clay army of 6,000 men and 1,400 chariots and cavalrymen. Each figure had different features and no two looked alike. This amazing tomb was discovered in 1974.

The Colosseum, Rome

The Colosseum is one of the most famous buildings in the world. The ancient Romans used it for contests between gladiators, spectacles where men fought animals, or animals fought each other. Mock sea battles were staged – the whole arena could be flooded in minutes. Most of the games were violent and the slaughter of animals was huge.

The Colosseum is a massive building seating about 50,000 spectators. Begun by the emperor Vespasian about AD 72, it was finished by his son, Titus, eight years later. It is a 48 m-high oval, built of stone and marble. The walls were strengthened with brick, concrete and metal frames. Under the arena were tunnels and rooms where prisoners, slaves and animals were kept before the performance.

▼ The maze of stones we see today in the bottom of the Colosseum was hidden by the arena's floor.

▲ The Colosseum is a masterpiece of Roman engineering, and it has been the model for many modern stadiums.

The games held in the Colosseum were outlawed in the fifth century AD, and the amphitheatre was abandoned. Over the centuries, the Colosseum became a quarry for the people of Rome, who stole the statues and stones to build houses and some of the city's grandest palaces.

Pont du Gard, Nîmes

Nowadays, we feel it is vital that all towns and houses should have a good water supply. Two thousand years ago, the ancient Romans thought the same. For every new city that they built, the Romans constructed aqueducts to provide it with a good supply of water.

At Nîmes in France, the old water supply was not enough for the new Roman city. So, Marcus Agrippa, who was in charge of Roman water works, built an aqueduct which brought water to the town from springs 50 km away.

The Romans usually buried the water channel below ground, but at one point the aqueduct had to cross the gorge of the River Gardon. Here the Romans built the magnificent Pont du Gard. It is 269 m long and carried water 49 m above the river and across the valley.

▼ The Pont du Gard stands near Nîmes in France. Its three levels supported a water channel at the top.

▲ The huge scale of the aqueduct can be seen by the size of the tourists who stand on the central level. The protruding bosses were left to carry scaffolding in case of repairs.

Just inside the walls of Nîmes, a circular pool with a settling tank and a series of sluices and outlets can still be seen. These were used to provide water to the city water system as it was needed.

Petra, Jordan

Petra is an ancient city in Jordan famous for the colour of the rock in which it is carved. Because of its colour, it is often called the rose red city. In fact, the rock is not only coloured red, but also pale blue, orange, yellow, purple and green.

Petra lies hidden in a narrow gorge. The buildings are carved into the cliff face with rooms disappearing into the rock. The Nabateans, an Arab people, settled on the site about 312 BC. The city stood on a trade route from Arabia to the Mediterranean, so Petra became a popular stopping place for weary travellers crossing the dry countryside.

After the Romans took over Petra in AD 106, the city continued to be prosperous. However, later the trading routes changed and the city's importance waned. Eventually it was abandoned. It was not found again until 1812.

▼ Much of Petra's buildings and water system are well-preserved. Many tombs were also cut into the rosy-coloured rock.

Petra is the Greek word for 'rock'. The name replaced the Biblical name of Sela. It was here, according to some stories, that Moses struck a rock and water poured out. This event took place during the forty years in the wilderness after the Israelites fled from Egypt.

Pyramid of the Sun, Teotihuacán

Teotihuacán was the greatest of all ancient Central American cities. With a population of over 200,000, it was the largest city of early Mexico. Two enormous pyramids rise high above the sun-baked city, rivalling those of ancient Egypt in size. They were built around the first century AD, and the city of Teotihuacán was planned around them. The Pyramid of the Sun is the city's most imposing building – it stands over 70 m tall – and on top is a temple.

Central American pyramids were used as temple platforms like the ziggurats of Mesopotamia (see pages 12 and 17), and not as tombs like the Egyptian pyramids (see pages 10–11). The Pyramid of the Sun rises up in several tiers. A wide stairway with very narrow treads leads to the top – it was designed to be climbed by the worshippers, probably with great effort. Near by stands the slightly smaller Pyramid of the Moon.

▲ The temple of Quetzalcóatl, the Feathered Serpent, lies to the south of the city of Teotihuacán. This sculpted head of a goddess decorates the outside along with other sculptures.

Teotihuacán was destroyed in the eighth century either by fire, or by invading people. For a time the city was probably the most powerful in the Americas. Its people had trading links with cities in the south-western USA, Mexico, Guatemala, Belize and Honduras. Teotihuacán existed at the same time as Tikal (see page 32) with which it also had important trading links.

▼ The Pyramid of the Sun stands halfway along the main street called the Avenue of the Dead.

The Pantheon, Rome

The Pantheon was built by the Emperor Hadrian in Rome, Italy, around AD 120 to 124 as a shrine to the gods. It is an impressive building showing what brilliant engineers the ancient Romans were.

Until this century, the Pantheon's dome was unbeaten in its span, which measures 43 m across. A dome of this size usually needed some support, but the Romans had mastered how to build arched roofs which did not need columns to hold them up. Although the Romans did not invent the arch, they were the first to realize its uses.

The oculus, or eye opening in the dome, allows light to pour into the Pantheon. Inside the floor and walls are made of brightly coloured marble. The Pantheon stands almost unchanged since it was finished, and gives the best impression of how a Roman building would have looked. When new, the Pantheon would have been far more sumptuous than we see it today, with statutes in the alcoves and a painted ceiling.

▼ The Pantheon is a circular building with a domed roof. It is one of the most well-preserved of ancient Roman buildings.

The Pantheon was made into a Christian church in AD 609. During the 1600s, the bronze roof was stripped away to be melted down in order to be used for decorating the inside of St Peter's Church in the Vatican City, and for making cannons for the castle of Sant'Angelo in Rome.

Hagia Sophia, Istanbul

Hagia Sophia, or Holy Wisdom, was built between AD 532 and 537, after the previous church on the site was destroyed in rioting. Its huge dome was supported by four enormous arches. This dome and the tops of the pillars were covered in beautiful mosaics, made of tiny pieces of glass, often picked out in gold and silver.

As Constantinople's cathedral, Hagia Sophia played an important role in the Byzantine Empire and all the emperors were crowned there. Sultan Mehmet II recognized this when the Ottoman Turks captured the city in 1453. He rode first to Hagia Sophia and announced it would be turned into a mosque. The Blue Mosque, another marvellous building, was built near by, but Hagia Sophia retained its importance. Now it is a museum.

▼ After Hagia Sophia was turned into a mosque, the four minarets were added to the building.

Hagia Sophia was built on the orders of Emperor Justinian, one of the greatest of the Byzantine Emperors, who codified laws and reconquered the old western empire.
When it was finished, the historian Procopius wrote that the dome appeared to have no foundation, but looked as if it was suspended from heaven on a golden chain.

Horyuji Monastery

Horyuji Monastery in Japan boasts the oldest wooden buildings in the world. They were built by Buddhist monks in the seventh century AD near the town of Nara, once the capital of Japan.

Horyuji divides into two areas: the Western Cloister and the Eastern Cloister. From the entrance, the Western Cloister leads to the Middle Gate whose pillars date from AD 670 when they were rebuilt after a fire. The original pillars were carved in AD 607.

The Pagoda and the Kondo, or main hall, are the two most famous buildings at Horyuji, although there are other buildings in the complex. The five-storey Pagoda has a series of tiled roofs each becoming smaller as the building rises. The top storey is exactly half the size of the bottom one.

The Kondo appears to have two floors but, in fact, it only has one, and the second roof is only there to make the building look taller.

▲ The Kondo Hall is one of the most famous temples at Horyuji.

Within Horyuji stands the Yumedono, or hall of dreams. This eight-sided building was constructed around AD 740 after the builder of Horyuji, Prince Shotoku, had a dream in which an angel appeared to him. The Yumedono contains a statue called the Secret Buddha, which is only on view in spring and autumn.

▼ The buildings of the Horyuji are entirely made of wood, including balconies, roofs, walls and pillars.

The Nazca Lines

Try and imagine enormously long lines and huge shapes and patterns drawn on the ground that are so big that you cannot tell that they are there. There are lines like these in the desert of Peru called the Nazca Lines. They stretch over hundreds of square miles. No one realized how much ground they cover until aeroplanes first began to fly over the desert in the late 1920s and 1930s.

The lines were first discovered in 1926. They were made between 100 BC and AD 700 by clearing away rocks leaving lighter soil showing underneath. The lines continue over hills and are still straight. Perfect straightness may have been achieved by using marker posts.

But why were they made? Some think they are linked with astronomy. Others believe they are religious pathways linking shrines and that the animal patterns are pictures of gods and spirits.

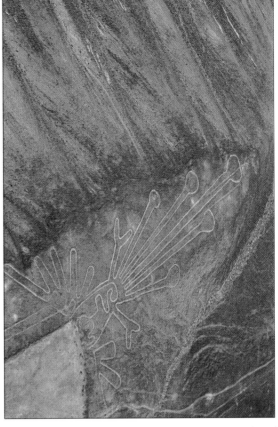

▲ Not all the lines in the desert are straight – some are in the shape of spiders, monkeys, hummingbirds, whales and people.

▼ Some lines stretch for miles crossing mountains and other rough country, but they remain straight.

The lines were called the Nazca Lines because some of the figures resembled those decorating pottery made by the Nazca people. They lived some time between 200 BC and AD 600 near the coast of Peru, and eventually became part of the Inca empire.

Temple of the Giant Jaguar, Tikal

The Maya civilization was one of the most brilliant of ancient Central America. It conjures up images of giant pyramids soaring above endless jungle, huge stones carved with intricate writings and bloody religious rites.

At its peak, in the eighth century AD, the city of Tikal in modern Guatemala, covered 120 sq. km and may have had a population of 55,000. Tikal was well organized with a covered market, courts for playing ball games, temple pyramids and underground food stores. Then, towards the end of the ninth century, the city was suddenly abandoned.

Tikal remained hidden and tangled in jungle plants for a thousand years. The Temple of the Giant Jaguar has now been cleared. It was built in AD 850 to 900 and towers into the sky with a steep staircase leading to the top. In the distance, other temples peer out of the tree tops into the blue sky.

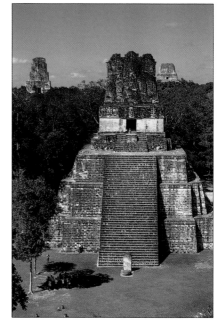

▲ The Temple of the Giant Jaguar rises an impressive 58 m above the canopy of jungle tree. At its heart, archaeologists found a tomb containing the skeleton of one of Tikal's rulers.

▼ Some of the temple buildings were plastered and painted on the outside. Today the remaining buildings are black with age with lichen growing on them.

The Maya built and rebuilt their cities constructing even greater monuments on the site of old ones. When buildings were knocked down, the huge carved pillars that stood nearby would also be demolished and new pillars put up. The pillars were carved with dates of family trees, wars and construction dates.

Temples of Ellora

Buddhists, Hindus and Jains came to Ellora in Central India. All these religious people place great importance on praying quietly and alone. Perhaps that is why they came to Ellora between AD 600 and 900. Buddhist monks arrived first at Ellora around AD 600. They carved out caves along a cliff face in which to live, and monasteries and magnificent temples in which to pray.

Around AD 765, the Hindus came to Ellora. They carved the grandest temple there, called the Kailasanatha. It is, in fact, a group of connected temples standing in a large pit. The rock was dug away from the top of the cliff leaving a central block. This was elaborately carved into temples, including the roofs and decorations. Five Jain temples were carved at Ellora around AD 850. The Indra Subha is the most well known, also cut from the solid rock.

▲ As well as being richly carved outside, the temples contain statues and carvings cut from the same rock.

▼ The Kailasanatha temple is carved into the rock and sits in a pit in the cliff.

The temples of Ellora were not known outside India until 1794 when they were seen by a British traveller. But it was another thirty years before anyone realized that the temples were becoming ruins, and a campaign was launched to preserve them. It is because of this work that the temples can be visited today.

Borobodur, Java

Borobodur in Java, Indonesia, is the most fantastic of Buddhist temples. It rises above the trees of the surrounding jungle like a huge fancifully iced cake. The temple was built in the eighth and ninth centuries AD by the Buddhist rulers called Saliendras.

Borobodur is pyramid-shaped and rises in steps. It has a square base of five walled terraces, which are decorated with thousands of carvings of Buddha's life. Above these are four very plain, circular terraces on which stand seventy-two bell-shaped stupas, or shrines. Each one holds a statue of Buddha. The terraces become smaller and smaller leading to the top, where there is a large stupa.

Buddhists must climb Borobodur in a particular way. Entering from the east and moving in a clockwise direction, the walk to the temple top symbolizes the path a person takes to reach spiritual maturity and understanding.

▶ The stupas on the top three tiers of the temple at Borobodur each contain a statue of the god Buddha.

▼ The temple of Borobodur rises up in different sized terraces. Each has a meaning symbolic to the followers of Buddhism.

In 1006, the population around Borobodur fled because of an earthquake and an eruption from one of the nearby volcanoes. The area seems to have been abandoned until 1814 when it was rediscovered. In the 1970s and 1980s, a major restoration of Borobodur was carried out using computer techniques to reposition the stones.

Terraces

Terraces climb the steep hillsides of many parts of the world, like steps built for a giant to reach the sky. They are flat areas cut into the hillside in order to plant crops. This is one of the most amazing ways in which people have shaped the landscape.

Terraces were first built in prehistoric times. The earliest clearings of the forest or hilltops were used for growing a few food plants or as defence points. These terraces began to appear around the world at roughly the same time.

Terraces prevent erosion, or the process whereby rain washes away the soil down the mountain. Most terraces are edged with stone walls which keep in the soil. In places where there are no stones, the walls are made of earth or grassy banks. The soil inside the 'step' of the terrace keeps rainwater in, making sure the plants are well watered.

▲ Terraces cover this valley in Peru and stretch as far as the eye can see, creating a patchwork of small fields to grow crops.

Glistening silver terraces, like a series of mirrors down a hillside, appear in parts of Asia where rice is grown. The terraces shine because they hold water. Rice grows in these trough-shaped terraces and it needs lots of water to grow. The water is supplied to the terraces by a complex series of channels.

▼ Hundreds of years ago, the native peoples of South America built terraces to grow crops for food. Today some of their terraces are still in use.

Igloo, Arctic

An igloo is an amazing structure because its dome shape requires no supports to keep it up. Igloos were once built by most of the native people living around the Arctic, the northern end of the world. They were used as temporary shelters on hunting trips. The Inuit of Canada lived in igloos all winter. Today no one lives permanently in an igloo.

Great skill is needed to build an igloo. The Inuit cut out large blocks of snow which had been packed hard by the wind and frost. In the past, a lamp was placed at the centre of the igloo for cooking, light and heat.

A ledge was built about 1 m above the floor for storage. Part of the ledge was covered with furs and used as a seat and bed. As the heat rose, the ledge kept the family inside warm by raising them closer to the top of the igloo.

▼ The Inuit used a long knife made of bone or metal to cut the blocks of snow. They were laid in a spiral pattern which wound upwards in smaller and smaller circles until the dome was complete.

▲ The entrance of some igloos was dug into the snow. A hole was made in the top of the igloo to let in fresh air, and sometimes a thin piece of ice was set in the wall to act as a window.

Several countires fall inside the Arctic Circle, and different native people live there. The Inuit are only one of the native peoples. Other Arctic people lived in tents or earth-walled homes all year round. Igloos were never built by the people of Alaska.

Yurt, Mongolia

On the mountain plains of Mongolia, where the wind can howl at extremely low temperatures, a series of round, white tents dot the ground. These are yurts, or *gers*, as the Mongols call them. They have been used for centuries, ever since the beginnings of the Mongol people, a date no one is quite sure of.

The *gers* make practical homes for the Mongols, most of whom are nomads spending the year following their goats, sheep, yaks, horses and camels to new pastures. The *gers* can be packed up and carried by several Bactrian camels to the next stopping point where the tent is reassembled. A *ger* is built on a round, wooden frame and covered with felt and animal skins. Brightly coloured rugs cover the inside, which is snug and warm from the heat of a stove. A hole in the roof allows smoke to escape.

▲ Most people in Mongolia today still live in their yurts or *gers*. Only people who live in towns own proper houses.

The walls of the yurt are made of wooden frames which can be folded shut for travelling. Once opened, the pieces are stretched to form a circle and tied together. The roof is made of poles attached to a wheel at the top. Felt and canvas are tied on to the frame providing insulation and protection from the harsh weather.

▼ In North America, the Native Americans developed the teepee or wigwam, based on much the same idea as the Mongol yurt.

Lingaraja Temple, Bhubaneswar

Bhubaneswar is a city on the coast of north-eastern India. Hundreds of years ago, it became a centre for the followers of the Hindu god, Shiva, and thousands of temples were built. Shiva is the god both of destruction and of reproduction and fertility. Of the 500 temples remaining, the Lingaraja temple is the best example of the styles of building used in the area.

Lingaraja Temple was built about AD 1000, and it has a more complex layout than other temples in the city. It contains a series of halls and rooms within a walled area, and the main tower is shaped like an extra tall beehive. The outside is covered with thousands of carvings and small sculptures of animals.

▲ The outside of the Lingaraja is decorated with many carvings of animals and gods.

The sides and pattern of the top of the temple show how the architects copied earlier shrines made of reeds, which were bunched together and tied in a knot at the top. The inside of the tower is reached by walking through the surrounding temple buildings. The space inside is actually quite small.

Only Hindus are allowed to enter the area inside the wall which surrounds the Lingaraja Temple. Each year a statue of a god from the temple is taken to a nearby lake and dipped in the holy waters.

◀ The Lingaraja temple uses the distinctive style of architecture typical of the area.

Cave dwellings, Cappadocia

In eastern Turkey strange cones, gleaming in the harsh sunlight, rise like large spikes on the hillside. During the fourth century AD, monks were urged by the Bishop of Caesarea, St Basil the Great, to settle there. The monks carved out caves which they linked up to form monasteries and churches. Here they lived and prayed. As the years passed, the caves grew in number.

By the thirteenth century the area was honeycombed with caves. More than 300 churches have been found carved into the rock, some with richly painted walls and ceilings. As many as 30,000 people may have used the churches.

In the fourteenth century, the religious community died out. Then, in the nineteenth century, monks again returned to live in the cones. They stayed until 1922. Today some caves are lived in by Turkish families, others are used as storerooms or stables.

▲ Many churches were carved into the volcanic rock which were often brightly painted inside. This fresco shows St George fighting the dragon.

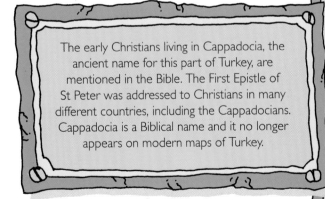

The early Christians living in Cappadocia, the ancient name for this part of Turkey, are mentioned in the Bible. The First Epistle of St Peter was addressed to Christians in many different countries, including the Cappadocians. Cappadocia is a Biblical name and it no longer appears on modern maps of Turkey.

◀ People have cut windows and doors into the cliff to light the caves dug behind. These are used as churches, houses and storerooms

Angkor Wat, Kampuchea

The huge temple of Angkor Wat stands in a clearing in the middle of the hot, steamy rainforest. Elsewhere, the plants have taken over the buildings of Angkor, the capital of the ancient Khmer Empire of Kampuchea, or Cambodia in South-East Asia. Angkor was built in a vast plain which the Khmer kings ruled over from the ninth to fifteenth centuries. Angkor Wat was built in the twelfth century, and it is the most impressive of the city's temples.

Angkor Wat is breathtaking and it is the largest religious building in the world. The main temple building is enclosed within a series of walls, its huge towers in the shape of lotus flower buds. The temple includes many statues, terraces, galleries, and courtyards, all arranged symmetrically. The outer covered gallery of Angkor Wat is richly carved with Hindu figures and myths. Angkor was abandoned in 1431.

▲ The whole of the temple is built using perfectly fitting stone blocks, which do not use cement or anything else to hold them together.

▼ The temple used to be surrounded by a huge moat which has now all but disappeared.

The temples of the Angkor area lay undiscovered until in 1860. But it was not until a century later that the size of the city was realized. It held over a million people and covered a huge area. The Khmers built a complex series of canals and enormous rectangular lakes, or reservoirs. This made water available, even in the dry season, to the city and to the surrounding fields.

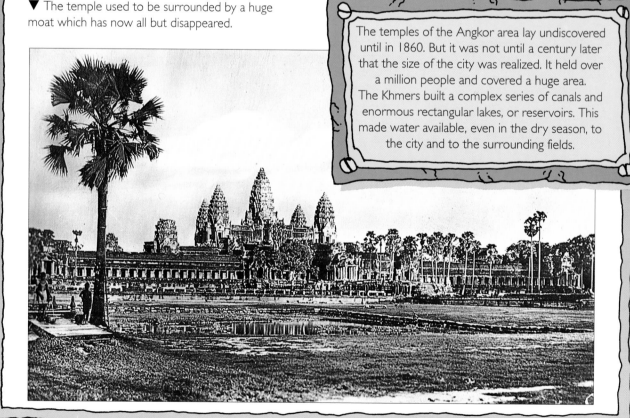

Mesa Verde, Colorado

The Anasazi people of the Mesa Verde built incredible dwellings high up, along canyon walls, in places which are almost unreachable. The cliff dwellings appear in south-western Colorado, in the USA. The Anasazi were an ancient people who built the remarkable cliff dwellings around the twelfth century. We do not know if they came here to be protected from the weather or from other tribes.

Cliff Palace is one of the largest cliff dwellings. It is really a village in the cliff. At the front are round semi-buried ceremonial rooms called kivas. Sheltering just beneath the cliff stand square brick buildings where the people lived. Behind these, built into the rockface, were the store rooms.

Spruce Tree House is another large ruin at Mesa Verde. It has around 115 rooms as well as kivas and it sits under the canyon's overhang. Not all cliff houses were large – some were very small.

▲ You can clearly see the circular ceremonial rooms as well as the brick buildings where the Anasazi people would have lived.

▼ At Spruce Tree House, the kivas still retain their roofs. A small entrance in the top leads into the kiva.

Spruce Tree House was discovered by two cowboys in a snow storm in 1888. Across the valley and hidden by trees, they spotted the village in the cliff. It had been empty for nearly 500 years. Mesa Verde National Park holds some of the most important cliff sites in North America. It is the only US National Park set aside to protect human-made structures.

The Leaning Tower, Pisa

The buildings of Pisa's cathedral, baptistery and bell tower look like pieces of a chess game standing in the square. They form one of the most famous groups of buildings in the world.

No other place has a tower quite like Pisa's. Begun in 1173, it was not finished until the fourteenth century. The tower has always tilted as the ground beneath it began to sink after only three stories were built. One architect after another tried to correct the tilt until, eventually, it was agreed that nothing could be done.

Accepting defeat, the remaining five stories were built. The cathedral is made of black and white marble set in lines and patterned with geometric shapes, which is typical of Pisan architecture. The Baptistery is also made of white marble like the tower.

▶ This ornate, circular building is the Baptistery.

▼ Despite recent attempts to stop the Tower leaning further, its 'lean' has not altered or stopped.

The bell tower leans 5 m to one side. A staircase winds up inside the tower, past the dizzyingly open arches to the bells at the top. A series of schemes have been tried to stop the tower from leaning further, and work is currently under way to at least save it from collapse.

Churches of Lalibela, Ethiopia

Hidden among the green olive trees, the eleven churches of Lalibela in northern Ethiopia suddenly appear. Usually people peer up at churches, but here they peer down. The churches stand in large ditches in the rock.

The elaborately carved churches are like enormous pieces of sculpture and were cut from the solid rock as were the temples at Ellora (see page 33). They were made in the late twelfth century during the reign of King Lalibela. Because the town became so popular, it was eventually renamed after the king. (Originally, it was called Roha.)

The churches were built to make the town into a religious centre – perhaps to rival Aksum as the most important Ethiopian city, or even Jerusalem. At one time they could only be reached by mule. Now Lalibela is easy to reach by road or air.

▼ There are two main groups of churches at Lalibela. They stand in pits which have been chiselled out of the rock. The churches are connected by underground passages.

▲ The House of Giorgis, or St George, is the only one of the churches at Lalibela to be carved in the shape of a cross.

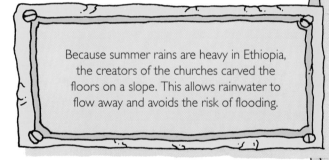

Because summer rains are heavy in Ethiopia, the creators of the churches carved the floors on a slope. This allows rainwater to flow away and avoids the risk of flooding.

Great Zimbabwe

Zimbabwe is the name of a country in southern Africa, but it is also a word used by local people for the ruins of stone buildings and huge walls that stand in a valley in the country.

Great Zimbabwe is the largest and grandest of these. It is a circular walled area containing houses and courtyards. The walls are 9 m high and about 5 m thick with large stones set along the top. Further down the valley there are many zimbabwes that are scattered over an area of about 24 hectares, including a temple surrounded by a wall and the remains of smaller buildings.

Great Zimbabwe was built between the eleventh and fifteenth centuries, but

▲ The high walls of Great Zimbabwe enclose the whole complex. They protected the houses and areas where craftsmen and traders would have worked.

Large stones of granite or soapstone were placed along the top of the wall of Great Zimbabwe. Some are carved in the shape of a bird with a crocodile looking up. Whether the stones were just decorations or had a special purpose is still not known.

little is known about its people. It was a thriving trading centre between gold fields to the west and the Indian Ocean to the east. But by the early sixteenth century, the people of Great Zimbabwe had left, perhaps because of famine or because of droughts.

◀ This cone-shaped tower stands in the temple enclosure. It is 9 m high and 15 m at the base. The tower is completely solid and smooth on the outside.

The Imperial Palace, Beijing

The Imperial Palace is so large that it is hard to imagine that it was all for one man, the emperor of China. The palace covers 101 hectares right in the centre of Beijing, China's capital (old name Peking). It was built between 1406 and 1420 after Emperor Rongluo (Jung-lo) moved the capital to Beijing in 1403.

A wide moat and high walls with watch towers at the corners surround the Imperial Palace – entrance is through the Wumen Gate. Inside, the complex is divided into two parts containing hundreds of buildings and courtyards.

The front part contains three large halls. The middle one, the Hall of Supreme Harmony, holds the Dragon Throne from which the emperor ruled. Today, the whole palace has been converted into a museum and is open to the public with many of the princes' houses turned into schools and offices.

The Imperial Palace is also called the Forbidden City, as no commoner or foreigner was allowed to enter without the special permission of court officials. In 1949, the Peoples' Republic of China converted the palace to museums and other public buildings.

▲ The Imperial Palace contains 9,000 rooms and housed the entire imperial court. As late as 1900, 10,000 servants, officials, slaves and princes lived there.

▼ The Hall of the Supreme Harmony rises impressively inside the royal complex of palaces. It is from this hall that the emperor used to rule.

Schwe Dagon Pagoda, Yangon

Glittering above Yangon in Myanmar (or Burma), the golden-spired Schwe Dagon Pagoda soars over the city. It is one of the most holy sites in the Buddhist world as it is built over eight of the Buddha's hairs. The pagoda is thought to have been built in 585 BC when it was only 8 m high. After work carried out in the fifteenth century, it rose to the height it is today – 99 m.

The building is an awe-inspiring sight as the bell-shaped pagoda is covered in gold. It sits on a base 60 cm high. Clustered around it are sixty-four smaller pagodas and four larger ones, all decorated in the most intense reds, greens, browns and golds. Adding to the riches of the pagoda, the very top is crowned with a bud encrusted with diamonds and other precious gems, but no one has ever been tempted to steal it.

▶ The golden pagoda sits surrounded by a cluster of smaller shrines on a platform paved with marble.

▼ This magniificent group of statues of the Buddha is housed within the Schwe Dagon Pagoda.

The eight hairs were given to two traders from Myanmar by the Buddha himself. They had sailed from their home and met the Buddha in India. On their return, the sacred gift was placed in a golden pagoda by the king on the Theinguuarra Hill where the Schwe Dagon Pagoda stands. This event has been faithfully recorded in Buddhist holy writings.

Machu Picchu, Peru

High in the Andes, the ruined Inca city of Machu Picchu nestles between two sharp mountain peaks. It is one of the few early towns of South America which has been found almost intact. Its remote position, 610 m high, may have saved the town from being looted by the Spanish who arrived in the region around 1532.

Machu Picchu is spectacularly perched on a narrow ridge. It was part of a chain of hill fortresses and it lies on an Inca road. The town contained about 150 houses as well as a semi-circular temple. Around the town a series of large steps, or terraces, descend the mountain, where the Incas grew food plants.

Machu Picchu may have been built around 1450 to 1500, not long before the Inca empire was destroyed by the Spanish. The town lay forgotten until 1911, when it was found by an American named Hiram Bingham.

▲ The intihuatana, or sun dial, is one of the most extraordinary features of the sanctuary area.

The Inca empire stretched for thousands of miles and, to ensure efficient communications, they built a network of roads stretching along the coast and through mountains.
The Incas used considerable engineering skill in constructing the 40,230 km of paved roads. They built bridges and causeways, too.

▼ Machu Picchu was built using stone blocks. No cement keeps the blocks together, instead they are skilfully placed tightly together.

Venice, Italy

Venice is one of the most unusual cities in the world as it lies in the middle of a seawater lagoon, with mainland Italy lying on one side and a narrow spit of land on the other. Venice is built on a series of islands criss-crossed by canals.

During the AD 400s, the first settlers of Venice fled to the marshy islands to escape Lombard barbarians who were invading Italy from northern Europe. There was soon no room on the small islands, but instead of returning to dry land, the Venetians enlarged the islands. They sunk wooden poles, or piles, deep into the mud of the lagoon and built their homes on stilts.

Discovering firm clay beneath the mud, they strengthened the wooden piles with layers of stone and planks creating blocks of land above water. Gradually the city grew and flourished.

▲ The city of Venice seems to float on the surface of the water as the waves of the lagoon wash the steps of the buildings.

In prehistoric times, whole villages in northern Italy had been built on wooden stilts in lakes. In Poland, too, a village was discovered in the 1930s which had been built on stilts over the wet marshy shores of Lake Biskupin. The village was constructed around 700 to 400 BC.

▼ Each year, floods and pollution damage the city. Many people have joined campaigns to save it.

St Basil the Blessed, Moscow

St Basil's Cathedral in Moscow, Russia, almost looks like a fairy castle. But its brightly coloured, onion-shaped domes and red stone all belong to a Christian church, although now it is only used as a museum. It was built in Red Square in 1555–61 on the orders of Tsar Ivan IV the Terrible as a holy offering to thank God for Ivan's recent victories in battle.

The cathedral's proper name is the Cathedral of the Intercession, but it has become known as the Cathedral of St Basil the Blessed after Basil the Russian holy fool who was buried in the church vaults. The actual cathedral building contains nine churches.

The central one is surrounded by eight smaller ones, which are the towers which we see from the outside. Each chapel has a differently patterned roof, and each is named after the saint on whose feast day Ivan had won a battle.

▼ The central tower is 33 m high. The eight smaller chapels surrounding it are linked by a raised gallery.

In the sixteenth century, the crypt of the church was used as a the state treasury. Knowing this, two noblemen decided to rob its contents in 1595. They had conjured up a clever plan to start fires around the city to distract the guards. Unfortunately, their plan failed and they were executed.

The Statues of Easter Island

The *moai*, or huge stone statues, of Easter Island are among the world's great mysteries. No one actually knows what purpose they served. There are more than 600 *maoi* scattered along the coast, blankly looking out at the Pacific Ocean. Most of them are 3.5–6 m tall, although some are 12 m high and weigh as much as 90 tonnes. Even today it would be difficult to raise such large statues.

The statues were made of volcanic rock and stood on platforms. Some had red, hat-like stones on their heads. They were carved by people who reached the island around AD 400. Some *maoi* are broken or are overthrown. Around 1680 there was a war between the two clans of islanders. Each group may have toppled its own statues to build bigger and better ones.

▲ Hundreds of giant statues are dotted about the island, although some are no longer standing upright.

The first people to settle on the very remote Easter Island were the Polynesians who sailed from other islands in the Pacific Ocean. They were skilled explorers and may have sailed to Easter Island to escape war or in search of food. The first Europeans arrived in 1722 on Easter Sunday, hence its name.

▼ The statues of Easter island were set on raised temple platforms called *ahu*.

St Peter's Church, Vatican City

St Peter's Church in the Vatican City towers above the rooftops. For Roman Catholics, St Peter's is the most important religious site (it is named after the leader of the disciples, St Peter). Its size is impressive – it can hold 50,000 people and covers 15,100 sq. m. Until 1989, it was the world's largest church.

The St Peter's we now see replaced an earlier church built by the Roman emperor Constantine in about AD 325. In 1506, Pope Julius II decided to demolish the old church and to build a new one on the same site. St Peter's is built in the shape of a cross and has a huge dome. The plans were changed many times during construction, as ten different architects worked on its design each changing the way it looked. St Peter's was eventually finished in 1615.

Bernini designed many features inside St Peter's. One was a massive bronze baldachino, or canopy, which stands 26 m over the main altar. It is said to mark the exact spot of St Peter's tomb. The metal for it was stolen from the roof of the Pantheon (see page 28) in 1633.

▼ One of the architects of St Peter's, Gian Lorenzo Bernini, created a fantastic setting for the church. He designed a huge piazza, or square, in front of St Peter's. The oval-shaped piazza contains two fountains and has two semi-circles of columns on each side.

St Peter's stands in the tiniest independent state in the world, the Vatican City, which is the home of the Pope, the head of the Roman Catholic church. It only covers 44 hectares, about the size of a city park. The Vatican City lies completely inside another city, Rome in Italy.

Taj Mahal, Agra

On the banks of the Jumma River, near Agra, in India is the Taj Mahal. It is one of the world's most beautiful and romantic buildings.

Shah Jahan, who ruled the Mogul Empire in the seventeenth century, was heartbroken when his favourite wife, Mumtaz Mahal, died in 1629. He decided to build a tomb in her memory. Building began in 1632 and 20,000 men worked daily to complete the building by about 1643. However, the surrounding buildings, mosque and walls were not finished until 1650.

The Taj Mahal is made of gleaming white marble. The building with its four minarets (prayer towers) stands on a platform 10 m high. Each face of the tomb has a huge arch which rises to the height of 33 m. Verses from the Qur'an, the Muslim holy book, frame the doorways, and a massive dome covers the centre of the building.

▲ Inside a central room contains two monuments to Mumtaz Mahal and Shah Jahan, decorated with precious stones inlaid in the marble. Screens cut with fine patterns protect the monuments. The bodies of the royal couple lie in a vault at garden level.

Shah Jahan planned to build a copy of the Taj Mahal in black marble on the other side of the river as his tomb, but he was never able to carry out his plan. His son seized power and imprisoned him. Shah Jahan died in 1658 and is buried beside his wife.

▼ The gleaming Taj Mahal tomb and its minarets are all entirely made from white marble blocks.

Himeji Castle, Nara

Not all castles look the same, although they all serve the same purpose – to protect those inside. Unlike the heavily walled castles of Europe, Japanese castles look very stylish with their up-turned roofs.

With its white walls and tall roofs, Himeji Castle is the largest and most elegant of the few surviving Japanese castles. It is sometimes called the White Egret, as it resembles the white egrets that nest on the banks of the Senba River. Huge ornamental fish were placed on the roof as charms to ward off fire,

which was no joke as most of the castle is made of wood.

The castle's defences were never tested in battle, but they are certainly impressive. Three moats – one inside the other – surround high curved stone walls scattered with watchtowers. Small holes can be seen all round the walls and towers, from which arrows and bullets could be fired at attackers.

The site where Himeji Castle stands has been fortified since 1333. The first castle was built there in 1580.
In 1681, this castle was rebuilt and expanded to form the present-day castle.

▼ About 387 tonnes of wood, 75,000 tiles weighing 3,048 tonnes and a huge number of large stones were needed to build the castle. The stones must have been difficult to find, for one stone is a huge millstone and some of the others are stone coffins.

Palace of Versailles, France

The palace of Versailles and its lavish grounds were built by King Louis XIV of France during the seventeenth century and conjure up images of luxury and wealth on an unimaginable scale. Inside, gold ornaments, rare antiques, paintings and sculptures decorate the palace's 1,300 rooms. Every imaginable comfort was included, and so it is not very surprising that Versailles took over forty years to complete.

The palace and its grounds were planned as a complete design. Two huge mirror-like ponds lie directly behind the palace, and a long cross-shaped canal stretches into the distance. The fountains were huge and spectacular. They used so much water that they could only be turned on for three hours at a time.

The grounds held 1,400 fountains, waterfalls, statues, ornaments and geometric flower beds and are probably the grandest gardens ever created.

▼ The palace of Versailles, seen reflected in one of the ponds, seems to stretch for miles it is so vast.

▲ Some of the fountains are truly stunning, the Bassin de Latone is filled with statues of turtles, frogs and Latona, the mother of the Greek god, Apollo. The fountain of Apollo has a life-sized statue of Apollo, with goddesses rising out of the water in a chariot pulled by three horses.

Water for the fountains and water displays in the grounds of Versailles was stored in specially made lakes, or reservoirs. These were supplied by a series of canals and aqueducts which brought water from high areas near Versailles.

Eddystone Lighthouse, Channel

Eddystone Lighthouse stands on rocks lashed by the waves of the English Channel. The lighthouse was built on Eddystone Rocks 22 km off the coast of Plymouth, England. It is not the only lighthouse to have stood there – the original one was the first-ever lighthouse to be built out at sea rather than on land. Designed by Harry Winstanley, it was built of wood in 1696–9, but was swept away in 1703 by a great storm.

The next lighthouse was made of wood and iron and lasted until 1755, when it was burnt down. Betweeen 1756 and 1759, John Smeaton built a third lighthouse entirely of stone. This stood until 1882 when the present one was built.

The lighthouse now standing on Eddystone Rocks is built 40 m above the water. Like most lighthouses today, it is no longer manned. They are run mechanically so no one has to spend long months living alone to tend the light. Every lighthouse gives out distinctive patterns of light. Some have a fixed beam and others flash, some even have red beams. Sailors can recognize a lighthouse by its beam.

◄ An old engraving shows the first lighthouse to be built at the Eddystone Rock.

▼ The Eddystone Lighthouse stands alone in the English Channel on a rock 22 kilometres from land.

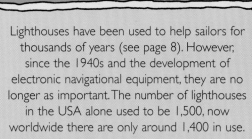

Lighthouses have been used to help sailors for thousands of years (see page 8). However, since the 1940s and the development of electronic navigational equipment, they are no longer as important. The number of lighthouses in the USA alone used to be 1,500, now worldwide there are only around 1,400 in use.

Transfiguration Church, Karelia

Although many buildings are made of wood, not many people would bother to bend the wood into curves and to add thousands of intricately cut wooden tiles. Most wooden buildings keep the straight lines of the timbers. However, on Kizhi Island in Karelia, Russia, stand some rather amazing wooden buildings.

The largest building on the island is the Russian Orthodox Preobranzhenskaya Church or the Church of the Transfiguration. It was built in 1714 of silvery-coloured aspen wood and stands 37 m tall. It has three tiers and twenty-two onion-shaped domes each decorated with tiny tiles and a large cross. The whole church was built without using any nails. Instead, the planks of wood have been slotted together.

Most old wooden buildings in Russia fell down a long time ago. However, the Church of the Transfiguration stands so far north that wood-boring beetles cannot survive the cold climate. This has saved the church from being gnawed away by insects.

▲ The Church of the Transfiguration stands on the shores of Lake Onega. It has been recognized by UNESCO as one of the world's architectural treasures.

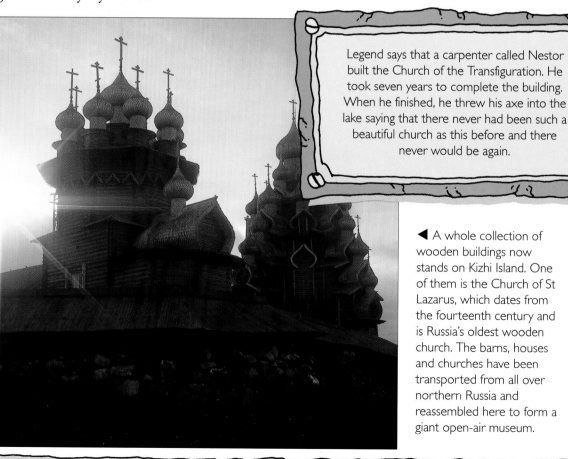

Legend says that a carpenter called Nestor built the Church of the Transfiguration. He took seven years to complete the building. When he finished, he threw his axe into the lake saying that there never had been such a beautiful church as this before and there never would be again.

◀ A whole collection of wooden buildings now stands on Kizhi Island. One of them is the Church of St Lazarus, which dates from the fourteenth century and is Russia's oldest wooden church. The barns, houses and churches have been transported from all over northern Russia and reassembled here to form a giant open-air museum.

Thames Tunnel, London

Every day, thousands of Londoners rush through a beautifully decorated tunnel. But it is all missed because the underground train speeds through the tunnel in just twenty five seconds and the decoration is covered by dirt.

The Thames Tunnel is now part of the London Underground system. It was designed in the nineteenth century by Marc Brunel and his son, Isambard Kingdom. At the time, the twin tunnels, which are 381 m long, were considered a spectacular engineering achievement.

To dig the tunnel, Marc Brunel devised a huge framework. It was divided into thirty-six cells each holding a miner who hacked away at the clay in front of him. When the miners had cut through the same quantity of clay, the frame was moved forward and the area covered with brick.

When the tunnel opened in 1843, only pedestrians could use it. In 1869, the East London Railway Company bought the tunnel to run trains under the river. It has been used for this ever since.

▲ The twin entrances of the Brunels' Thames Tunnel as it appeared in the days when people using it walked through.

Isambard Kingdom Brunel (1809–59) was a most original inventor. His famous works include the Suspension Bridge over the Avon Gorge in Bristol, England, which was completed in 1864. He also built the first propeller-driven, ocean-going iron ship in 1843. Brunel is best known for his work on the Great Western Railway in England.

◄ In the first few years of opening thousands of people walked through the tunnel, but later its popularity grew less as it was difficult for many horse-drawn carriages to enter.

The Crystal Palace, London

The Crystal Palace is probably the largest greenhouse ever built. We have all seen glasshouses in gardens or large commercial ones used to grow crops. But none surpass the enormous scale of the Crystal Palace. It was built for an exhibition organized by Prince Albert, Queen Victoria's husband, held in London between May and October 1851.

The Crystal Palace was designed by Joseph Paxton. It was a remarkable structure, not only because of its size, but also because it was a prefabricated building. It consisted of a frame of iron rods holding walls of clear glass.

After the exhibition, Crystal Palace was taken apart and was rebuilt in south London to a more elaborate design. It became a venue for shows, exhibitions, concerts and other entertainments. On the night of 30 November 1936, it was almost totally burnt down. What remained was left standing until 1941.

▼ During the exhibition, 1,400 exhibitors came from around the world and six million people visited the displays.

▲ When the Crystal Place moved to south London, it was set in elaborate gardens. It was still a popular destination and a railway nearby brought visitors from all over London.

Joseph Paxton was knighted for his work on the Crystal Palace. He was well known for building houses of iron and glass. He designed one in 1840 to hold plants at Chatsworth, a grand country house belonging to the Duke of Derbyshire. In 1850, Paxton built another glasshouse there to house the duke's rare lilies.

Suez Canal, Egypt

The Suez Canal stretches across a small piece of land called the Isthmus of Suez, which separates the Mediterranean Sea from the Red Sea. Built from 1859 and 1869, it offered ships a much shorter route from Europe to India without having to sail around Africa.

Because of its importance as an inter-ocean highway and short cut, it has played an important part in recent history – there have been several major disputes over it.

The canal stretches for 190 km from Port Said to Suez. There are no locks on the canal as there is little difference in the level of the Mediterranean Sea and the Red Sea. The canal has been enlarged several times since it opened, but most of it can still only take a single lane of traffic.

▲ The Suez Canal does not in fact run in a straight line. It also links two lakes as it cuts through the Isthmus of Suez.

Thousands of years ago canals connected the River Nile to the Red Sea. During the seventh century, a canal was cut to join the Red Sea to the Mediterranean. When Napoleon Bonaparte invaded Egypt in 1798, he saw the advantages of a canal across the Isthmus of Suez, but it was a French diplomat and canal builder, Ferdinand de Lesseps, who carried out the plan.

▼ When the canal was built it was 8 m deep, 22 m wide at the bottom, and 70 m wide at the surface. Today, all the measurements have more than doubled as the canal has been enlarged to carry modern ships.

Neuschwanstein Castle, Bavaria

Think of a fairy-tale castle and you will picture one like Neuschwanstein in Germany. It perches on a rocky ledge overlooking a lake and surrounded by forest. King Ludwig II of Bavaria (now part of Germany) started the castle in 1869, but when he died in 1886 it was not quite finished.

Ludwig had a mania for castle-building and also built two others. He was a big fan of the composer Richard Wagner, and the castle was inspired by Wagner's operas. The king also added his own ideas about the old stories the operas were based on, to the design of the castle. Ludwig increasingly shut himself away in the fantasy worlds of his castles. Eventually they led to his downfall because he had spent vast amounts of money – his own and the state's – in building the castles.

▲ Neuschwanstein lies in the Bavarian Alps. It is one of the most popular tourist attractions in Germany.

The largest castle which is still lived in is Windsor Castle in England. It was built in the twelfth century, and the British royal family still use the castle. The largest ancient castle is the ninth century Hradcany Castle in Prague, Czech Republic, which covers 7 hectares.

▼ The Singers' Hall is a particularly striking room in the castle. It is decorated with scenes from the Parsifal legend which Richard Wagner used for one of his operas, *Parsifal*.

Statue of Liberty, New York City

Few sights inspire such emotion as the Statue of Liberty. To many, it is the very symbol of the USA. The towering statue of a robed woman holding a torch stands on Liberty Island in New York Harbour. The figure is actually called 'Liberty Enlightening the World', and is made of copper sheets hammered into shape and riveted together.

The statue was given to the USA by the people of France in 1884 to commemorate the centenary of the American Declaration of Independence. Work on the statue, which was made in sections, began in 1875, and it arrived in the USA in 1885. The pedestal on which it stands was donated by the American people, and completed in April 1886. Six months later the statue was assembled and erected in position.

An internal framework of iron and stainless steel holds the statue upright. This was designed by Gustave Eiffel, the French engineer who created the Eiffel Tower (see page 62). Two spiral staircases wind up to the crown on the statue's head, which houses a viewing platform.

▲ The Statue of Liberty is one of the largest statues ever built, and stands over 46 m high. Three hundred sheets of copper were used to cover the frame.

▶ Visitors can climb up inside the statue to the crown. They are not allowed inside the torch. In the 1980s, when the statue underwent repairs, the gold-coloured torch was replaced with a new one.

The Statue of Liberty shows a proud woman holding a glowing torch. She wears a crown with seven spikes that stand for the light of liberty shining over the seven seas and seven continents. Her left hand holds a tablet engraved with the date of the American Declaration of Independence. A broken chain at her feet represents victory over tyranny.

Eiffel Tower, Paris

The Eiffel Tower is the one thing everyone looks for when they visit Paris. Even today it stands above the city's other buildings. From a distance, the tower looks slender and delicate, but moving closer it seems like an iron monster and its arches seem to cover whole streets.

The tower was designed by Gustave Eiffel for a Centenary Exhibition in 1889 to celebrate the French Revolution. A competition was held to build a suitable monument for the fair, and Eiffel's entry won. Reaction to the tower was fierce and many people did not want it at all. Nothing like it had ever been built. In less than two years, the Eiffel Tower was finished.

The tower rests on four arches and rises 301 m. Lifts and stairs climb up the legs to the top. For years it was the tallest building in the world until, in 1930, it was overtaken by the Chrysler Building (see page 69).

▲ We are so used to the Eiffel tower being part of the Paris skyline that we cannot imagine it not being there. This picture from 1888-9 shows it under construction.

Gustave Eiffel was a clever engineer specializing in metal construction. He designed several steel-arched bridges, as well as the iron and steel framework inside the Statue of Liberty in New York City (see page 61).

◄ The Eiffel Tower contains restaurants and a weather station, and since 1953 it has been used to transmit TV programmes.

In 1986 the tower's floodlighting was replaced. The new lighting is placed inside the tower's iron structure, so even at night the tower looks impressive.

The Pier, Southend-on-Sea

The first pleasure piers in Britain were built in 1812–14, and by 1895 there were seventy pleasure piers in England and Wales. In the nineteenth century, piers provided an exclusive walking space for the wealthier holiday-maker. Nowadays, they are associated with cheap entertainments. Pleasure piers were perched on a lattice-work of spindly iron or wooden legs pointing out to sea from shore. They had a wooden walkway with a pavilion or some other building on the end.

Southend-on-Sea pier was built when sea resorts near London were competing against each other for trade. It was to be the pier to outdo all others. Begun in 1830, and extended in 1845, it was 2 km long. But the owner ran out of money, and in 1875 the local authority took over its running. In 1888–90, they rebuilt it in iron. The present pier is 2.15 km long.

▲ Holiday-makers took daily strolls on the pier. Like many other nineteenth-century piers, the pier at Southend-on-Sea also served as a landing stage for steamers, some carrying passengers from London.

The resort with the most piers is Atlantic City in the state of New Jersey, USA – perhaps the only place outside Britain to have pleasure piers. It had eight piers of which only five remain. Piers used for mooring or fishing are found around the world.

▼ Southend Pier is the longest pleasure pier in the world and stretches over a mile into the sea. It was famous for the train which ran along it. The train now only travels part of the length of the pier.

Corinth Canal, Greece

The Corinth Canal cuts through a short piece of land, called the Isthmus of Corinth, and it provides a short cut between the Aegean and Ionian Seas. From a distance, the canal looks like a small strip of water, but as a ship gradually approaches and enters, its scale becomes apparent. However it is too small to take the supertankers and container ships of modern shipping.

The canal is only 5.5 km long, but it is 79 m deep, the deepest cut canal in the world and one of the very few that is cut through solid rock, so that the ship remains at sea level all the time.

The idea for a link between the Aegean and the Ionian Seas dates from ancient times, but no digging was started until during the reign of the Roman emperor

Nero in AD 67. The enormous project was largely carried out by Jewish prisoners from the Roman colony of Judaea. Work stopped in AD 68 because of disturbances elsewhere in the Empire.

It was not until the 1890s that the technology became available to complete the work. A French company began building it in 1892 and the Greek government completed it in 1893. It is spanned by a road and a railway bridge.

There are various descriptions of how work was started on the canal in AD 67. Most agree that Emperor Nero personally dug the first hole, but they are divided as to whether he used a gold or a silver shovel.

▶ The Corinth Canal cuts through a narrow strip of land in mainland Greece connecting the Aegean and Ionian Seas.

Tower Bridge, London

The twin towers of London's Tower Bridge are among the city's best-known sites. The bridge was built in the 1890s and was opened for use in 1894.

Like many bridges, it has a road and walkways running over it, but what makes it extra special is that the roadway opens up to allow tall ships to sail further into the city of London. Unfortunately, today there are not many tall ships left and the bridge only opens a few times each week. When the bridge was first completed, it was opened 600 times in the first month.

The style of the towers is probably grander than any bridge in the world, symbolizing Britain's once great empire and the busy river Thames. Inside, the towers contain several rooms.

The walkways over Tower Bridge were closed to the public from 1909 to 1982. Sadly, it had become a popular spot for people attempting suicide by plunging into the Thames.

▼ Tower Bridge opens up to allow tall ships to sail further up the River Thames.

The Canal, Panama

The Panama Canal is one of the world's great engineering feats. It cuts though a slim piece of land, or isthmus, dividing the Atlantic from the Pacific Ocean. At its narrowest point, the canal is 152 m wide, and is 82 km long. Ever since Rodrigo de Bastidas trekked across the isthmus to discover the Pacific Ocean in 1513, people have dreamed of building a waterway to connect the two oceans. However, early attempts in the nineteenth century were disastrous.

A French company attempted to dig a canal in 1882 – it was carefully planned by Ferdinand de Lesseps, who had headed construction of the Suez Canal (see page 59). But the scheme ran out of money and tropical illness killed hundreds of workers. In 1889, the company went bankrupt, and another French company took over.

In 1903, the US government bought the land, and digging began again in 1906. Over 43,400 men were employed using steam shovels and dredges to cut through jungle, hills and swamps. The first ship sailed through the waterway in 1914. Today, the Panama Canal is one of the busiest shipping canals in the world.

▲ The Panama Canal allows ships to take a short cut from the Atlantic to the Pacific Ocean without sailing around South America. The canal has three sets of locks which raise and lower ships from one level of water to another.

It must have been nightmarish for the diggers as they cut through jungle, suffering mosquitoes and other biting insects in the humid heat. Huge amounts of earth were removed, all without the aid of the machinery we have today. The Chagres River was damned to form Gatum Lake, the canal locks were constructed and solid rock was cut away to form the Gaillard Cut.

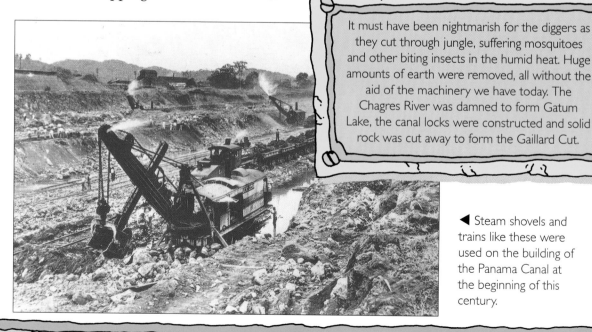

◀ Steam shovels and trains like these were used on the building of the Panama Canal at the beginning of this century.

FIAT Lingotto Factory, Turin

The great Italian automobile manufacturer, FIAT (short for Fabbrica Italiana Automobili Torino), was founded in 1899 by Giovanni Agnelli. The company soon expanded and became successful. By 1916 the company was a major supplier of the Italian armed forces and desperately needed more space.

Agnelli commissioned Giacomo Matté-Trucio to design and build for FIAT a state-of-the-art factory. He designed a re-inforced concrete building, the first in Italy. It was five storeys high, 500 m long and had a racing test track on the roof. Many of Agnelli's ideas were included in the final design. FIAT developed racing car engines – the famous 405 engine was developed and tested at Lingotto in 1923. Today FIAT also produces farm and railway equipment and aeroplane engines.

▲ A section of the assembly line in 1934 shows the popular FIAT car, the Balilla, going into production.

Giovanni Agnelli was an intellectual socialist. He thought FIAT should provide transport for ordinary people, as well as giving jobs to hundreds of workers. FIAT provided health clinics, convalescent homes, schools and other benefits for its workers and their families.

▼ Completed in 1920, FIAT's Lingotto factory featured a racing test track on the roof.

The Sagrada Familia, Barcelona

For a half-finished building, the Church of the Sagrada Familia, or Holy Family, in Barcelona, Spain, has not done badly as it is among the world's most famous sites. This bizarre building looks as if it has been hand-moulded from soft clay, but it is, in fact, made of red stone.

It was designed and built by Antoni Gaudí i Cornet. He devoted his life to the building – he started it in the early 1880s and it was still not finished at his death in 1929.

The church's four hollow towers soar skywards looking like large ant hills pierced with hundreds of openings. The tops of the towers form intricate shapes and are decorated with pieces of coloured tiles. A cross surrounded by balls crowns each tip. The towers almost have the appearance of octopus legs, the whole building looks as if it could be alive as it has no straight lines.

▲ From the walls of the Church of the Sagrada Familia sprout all sorts of gargoyles, lizards, snakes and salamanders, among the many other sculptures.

Gaudí designed other sites and buildings which use curves and are richly decorated with pieces of coloured tiles, marble and pottery, such as the Casa Batlló (built in 1905–7) and the Park Güell (built in 1900–14).

◀ Today, work is being done to complete the two central towers and the main building. It is estimated that it will take at least another fifteen years to complete the church.

Chrysler Building, New York

The early skyscrapers of the twentieth century can be seen as the modern equivalent of the monuments that ancient rulers built for themselves. They were built to show off a person's power and wealth. The Chrysler Building was commissioned by Walter P. Chrysler, the founder of the Chrysler Corporation, which manufactured cars. The Chrysler Building was built in 1926–31, and stands in New York City, USA. It was the first skyscraper to rise over 305 m.

The building is designed in the Art Deco style of the time. It is geometric and streamlined, and one of the style's most popular patterns, the sunburst, was used for the arrangement of the windows at the top. Adding to its appeal, the top of the building shines as the sunlight reflects on it, for it is covered in stainless steel.

▲ From the sixty-first floor, metal eagle gargoyles stare on to the street below. Walter P. Chrysler asked for them to look like radiator cap ornaments as a reminder of his great car-making empire.

The spire at the top was added late in the skyscraper's construction to make it the world's tallest building. But it was a short-lived record, for the Empire State Building, which was finished only a few months later, was taller.

◀ The Chrysler Building rises 319 m above the New York City skyline. The distinctive sunburst pattern of windows at the top make it easily recognizable.

Afsluitdijk, Netherlands

The people of the Netherlands have been reclaiming areas of their country from the North Sea for centuries. Very early on, the people living around a large inlet on the coast, the Zuiderzee, began draining areas of land. By 1667, so much land was being drained that it was thought a good idea to dam the Zuiderzee to create one large artificial island. However, the technology available at that time limited the action which could be taken.

No one came up with a possible plan until 1916. Then Cornelis Ley designed a huge dam separating the Zuiderzee from the North Sea. It is called the Afsluitdijk, or Enclosing Dam. It was built between 1927 and 1932, and it is 30 km long. When the sea dam was finished, the area behind it became a freshwater lake called the IJsselmeer. Huge areas of land were drained creating polders, land which has been reclaimed from the sea.

▲ The Afsluitdijk was built to include various locks allowing barges and boats to go in and out. However, many towns around the old Zuiderzee which were busy fishing ports are now empty of life.

The Afsluitdijk Dam is very long, but there are longer. When the Yacyreta Dam across the Paraná River on the Argentina–Paraguay border is finished in 1998, it will be the longest dam in the world. It will measure 69 km in length.

▼ The Afsluitdijk, or Enclosing Dam, is not very high – only 7.5 m above sea level. A road and bicycle path run along the top of the dam.

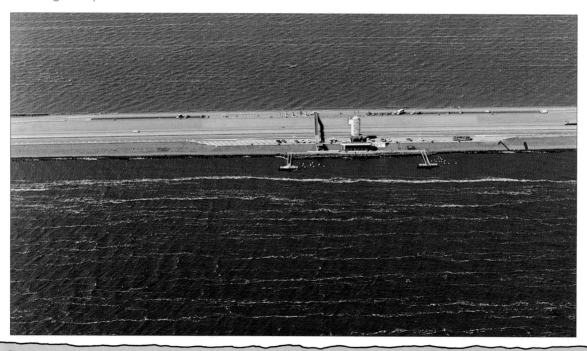

Golden Gate Bridge, California

The red towers of the Golden Gate Bridge are visible from much of the city of San Francisco in California, USA. The Golden Gate Bridge is thought by many to be the most beautiful bridge in the world, and it certainly has one of the most spectacular settings. It spans the entrance to the San Francisco Bay joining the city of San Francisco with northern California.

The bridge took just over four years to design and build. It opened in 1937, thus making ferry crossings across the bay unnecessary. The bridge hangs from two cables which are 94 cm thick. The main span between the two towers measures 1,280 m, and it is still one of the longest spans in the world. The towers are the tallest bridge towers in the world and are 227 m high.

It takes half an hour to walk the length of the bridge from the city of San Francisco on one side, to Marin County on the other. Sadly the bridge is a favourite place for people to commit suicide from.

In 1987 the Golden Gate Bridge was fifty years old, and quarter of a million people (a third of San Francisco's population) arrived for a party at sunrise to celebrate the bridge's birthday. The strong winds that day and the huge numbers of people standing on the bridge caused it to buckle slightly under the weight.

▼ The Golden Gate Bridge was the first really massive suspension bridge to be built. The bridge towers look especially eerie when fog shrouds the bridge and only the tops of the towers are visible as if floating in mid-air.

Mount Rushmore, South Dakota

The faces on Mount Rushmore stare out on to the countryside of the Black Hills of South Dakota in the USA. Unlike other huge sculptures, such as the statues on Easter Island (see page 50), or the Sphinx in front of the Great Pyramid at Giza in Egypt, which were carved hundreds of years ago, these images do not belong to another time. The faces on Mount Rushmore are relatively modern as they were only carved between 1927 and 1941.

The faces of four US presidents appear on the cliff face. They are George Washington, Thomas Jefferson, Theodore Roosevelt and Abraham Lincoln. Each of the heads is about 18 m high, which is as tall as a five-storey building. Designed by Gutzon Borglum, the faces were cut in an easier way than those of the ancient sculptors, as the workers used air drills, pneumatic chisels and dynamite.

▼ The cliff where the four presidents are carved rises 1,745 m, and the faces are carved near the top of the rocks.

The nose of one of the Mount Rushmore faces is so large that it is longer than the whole head of the Sphinx in Egypt. (see page 11).

Grand Coulee Dam, Washington

Grand Coulee Dam stands near the head of the Grand Coulee, a steep gorge where the Columbia River once flowed in Washington, USA. A wall of concrete holding back the waters of the Columbia River. This is the largest concrete dam in the world and the greatest source of hydroelectric power in the USA.

It is the largest and most complex of a series of dams on the Columbia River. The dam was begun in 1933 and it was opened in 1942, although since then it has undergone additional construction. The Grand Coulee Dam is 1,272 m long, and it takes nearly twenty minutes to walk from one side to the other. It is 152 m wide at the base and 168 m high. So much concrete was used that four pyramids could have been built with it.

▲ The Grand Coulee Dam was opened in 1942 and it remains the world's largest concrete dam.

The most massive dam, measured by volume, is New Cornelia Tailings on Ten Mile Wash in Arizona, USA. It has a volume of 209.5 million cubic metres. This will soon be overtaken by another dam, Syncrude Tailings Dam, near Fort Murray in Canada. It will be the largest volume dam with 540 million cubic metres.

▼ Water gushes through the Grand Coulee Dam, Washington State in the USA, which powers the turbines to produce electricity.

The Pentagon, Virginia

The Pentagon Building is the headquarters of the US Army, Navy and Air Force, and also holds the Office of the Secretary of Defence. It is a huge building and, as its name suggests, has five equal sides (a pentagon is a five equal-sided shape).

When it was built it covered the largest floor space of any office building in the world. It stretches over 14 hectares including a central court, which covers 2 hectares. About 23,000 people work there every day.

▼ The Pentagon lies on the banks of the Potomac River in Arlington, Virginia, directly across from the US capital, Washington DC. The Pentagon also has a radio and television station and a heliport. Car parks around the building can hold about 10,000 vehicles and cover 27 hectares.

The Pentagon consists of five pentagon shapes – one within the other – and all of five stories each, joined by ten spoke-like corridors. Building work started in 1941 and finished sixteen months later. It was purpose-built to bring together the scattered offices of the US War Department.

The Pentagon Building has one of the world's largest private telephone systems and it can handle 200,000 calls a day. It also has the largest pneumatic tube system to send messages, consisting of about 24 km of tube. It may also operate the largest food service in the world, serving over 15,000 meals daily to the people who work there.

Pan-American Highway

Imagine one road that runs from the edge of the USA, through Central America and most of South America. The Pan-American Highway achieves this incredible link. People had talked of building a Pan-American railway in the nineteenth century, but it was not until 1923 that a highway was seriously considered and organization of the system began. By 1950 most of the road in South America was open.

The Pan-American Highway does not just run in a straight line from the US–Mexico border through to Chile, but it also connects east and west South America. It links seventeen capitals of South American countries.

The road provides a route for agricultural products and raw materials to be transported. Although the Pan-American Highway is sometimes described as running all the way from the US state of Alaska, the road does not actually begin this far north.

The Highway is interrupted at the Darien Gap in Panama. Here, jungle blocks the path of the road for about 161 km. Motorists usually put their cars on a ship to cross to Venezuela or Colombia where the Highway starts again.

▲ The highway crosses many different types of environment, including deserts, conifer and tropical forests and mountains.

▼ The Pan-American Highway system covers 47,515 km of road and provides a link between North and South America.

Guggenheim Museum, New York

The Solomon R. Guggenheim Museum in New York City, USA, sits on a street corner looking like a huge white spring. This stunning, unique structure was completed in 1959. The outside of the building spirals upwards and outwards. The inside curves as well – a ramp leads to the six levels. The middle of the spiral forms an open space lit by a glass dome.

The museum houses the Solomon R. Guggenheim collection of modern art, after which the museum is named. Many of the works are hung from metal arms making them appear to float in the air. Traditionally, museums had exhibited works of art around the walls of large rooms or halls. The Guggenheim broke away from traditional practice.

The building is completely plain on the outside with only the museum name as an ornament. Smooth white concrete covers the walls, making them feel more like a giant sculpture than a building.

▲ Inside the Guggenheim, a long spiral walkway leads to the different sections, or floors of the gallery.

The Guggenheim Museum was designed by Frank Lloyd Wright, one of the USA's most original architects. He had a long career which began in the 1880s and included Robie House and Falling Water House, both in the USA. Frank Lloyd Wright continued working until his death in 1959.

▼ The Guggenheim Museum stands on a corner in New York City. It is unlike any other building.

Arecibo Observatory, Puerto Rico

The Arecibo Observatory in Puerto Rico, an island in the Caribbean, is so huge it can be see from a jumbo jet. However, on the ground, it is almost completely hidden, as it sits neatly tucked away into a large hole in the ground, known as a sink hole.

The observatory, which was built in the early 1960s, houses the world's largest radio telescope. It has the largest radio dish spanning 305 m across. The dish is made of almost 40,000 perforated aluminium mesh panels, which focus incoming radio waves on to a moveable antenna positioned above the dish's surface.

This antenna can be moved in any direction, making it possible to track an object across the sky. The radio telescope is so sensitive that it can detect objects 13 million light years away.

▼ The large radio telescope listens to messages from space, perhaps one day hoping to pick up messages from another life source. The observatory at Arecibo is run by the American Cornell University. It has been in the news on various occasions for major astronomical discoveries.

Puerto Rico lies near the Equator, which makes it an ideal setting for an observatory for the tracking of planets, pulsars and other objects in space.
NASA recently spent US$100 million here for its Search for Extra-Terrestrial Intelligence (SETI) programme.

Kiev Dam, Ukraine

The mighty Dneiper River is the fourth longest river in Europe. It rises near the city of Smolensk in Russia and flows for about 2,200 km south through Belarus and Ukraine, finally flowing into the Black Sea. The Dneiper is an important river for industry, transporting cargo and producing energy.

Immense dams and hydroelectric plants operate along the river supplying energy and water to industrial areas. One – the Dneproges Dam – provides electricity for most of the mines. Perhaps the most impressive is the Kiev Dam, which is the longest dam in the world. Built in 1964, it measures a fantastic 41.2 km along its crest, or top.

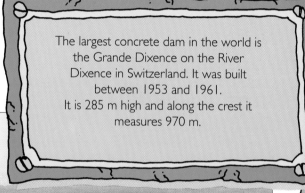

▲ Water flooding out through the sluice gates of one of the Dneiper's many dams.

▼ The Dneiper river runs through three republics and flows past the city of Kiev, the capital of the Ukraine.

The largest concrete dam in the world is the Grande Dixence on the River Dixence in Switzerland. It was built between 1953 and 1961.
It is 285 m high and along the crest it measures 970 m.

Vehicle Assembly Building, Florida

The Vehicle Assembly Building (VAB) in Florida is no ordinary factory – it is not motor cars or trucks that are made on its assembly line, but rockets and space shuttles. It was here that the *Apollo* spacecraft and the *Saturn V* moon rockets were constructed in the 1960s and 1970s.

The VAB is at Cape Canaveral, at the Kennedy Space Center. This fascinating place has been the home of the USA's space programme since the late 1950s. The VAB was built between 1963 and 1965, but it was not until October 1968 that the first manned *Apollo* flight was made with a three-man crew. In July 1969, the *Apollo II* spacecraft put the first men on the moon. The final *Apollo* flight was in 1972.

In 1981, the space shuttle made its first voyage from Cape Canaveral. This really marked the beginning of space travel as this craft was designed to last for years and it could be reused.

▼ The VAB covers one of the largest spaces in the world. Space shuttles are made here before being carried by Crawler Transporters to the launch pad.

VAB was once the world's largest building (the Boeing Company's main aircraft assembly plant at Everett, Washington, USA, now holds this record). Over the years, VAB been expanded and can now hold twice the amount it could when it first opened. Recent expansions were to prepare for the production of the new 777 airliner. The building now covers 415 hectares.

Rance River Barrage, France

For many years scientists have wondered whether the power of the sea could be turned into energy that we can use. Potentially, the sea is an everlasting, safe, clean and cheap source of power.

In 1966, a huge barrage was constructed across the mouth of the River Rance in France for a tidal power station. In the mouth of a river or in a narrow bay, the water rushes in and out as the tide rises and falls. The Rance Barrage does not stop the sea from flowing through, it contains huge pipes which let water pass.

Inside the pipes are turbines – large motors which spin as the water gushes through when the tide comes in. These turbines drive generators which produce electricity. When the tide flows out again, the turbines spin once more. The Rance River Barrage has thirty-eight turbines.

▲ At high tide the sea gushes into the river and drives the turbines in the Rance Barrage.

Tidal power stations only work well where there is a large rise and fall in the tides, and not many places have this.
An experimental tidal power station has been built in the Bay of Fundy in Canada. Here there is a rise and fall in tides of about 15 m, which is one of the biggest in the world.

▼ Strong sea tides made the Rance Barrage possible as the river flows out into an area of sea which has large changes in tide levels.

Geodesic Dome

The architect, R. Buckminster Fuller, had a clever idea for a structure which was easy, light and fast to erect. His design was based on a framework of tetrahedrons (solid pyramid shapes). You may have made models of them at school, perhaps using drinking straws as the framework. Did you ever wonder what the use of it all was?

A sphere with a framework of tetrahedrons would make a very strong structure as the weight would be spread equally throughout. Buckminster Fuller made domes in a variety of different materials and sizes which could be used for all sorts of purposes.

The Rotunda Building of the Ford Company in Dearborn, Michigan, USA, has a geodesic dome for the roof. This was built in 1953. The Ford Company chose a geodesic dome as it weighed a lot less than any other form of dome and the building needed a lightweight covering because it could not support the weight of a heavy dome. A ball-shaped geodesic dome was used for the US Pavilion at Expo '67 at Montreal in Canada.

R. Buckminster Fuller's geodesic dome has been used by the US Army instead of tents as they needed fewer parts, they were faster to put up and lighter to carry. The domes can be made in any material and there is no limit to size.

▼ A dome like the Expo '67 one can cover large areas and it can be quickly constructed. This one was made of lightweight steel tubes and plastic, balloon-shaped panels.

Jet d'Eau, Geneva

Rocketing up into the sky with an astounding whoosh, and spraying everything nearby with water is the amazing fountain called the Jet d'Eau in the lakeside harbour of Geneva, in Switzerland. The water rises in a single jet reaching 145 m, before crashing down with an enormous roar on to the surface of Lake Geneva.

Geneva is famous as a city of international conventions and a venue for peace negotiations and inter-government talks. Many worldwide companies and organizations have their headquarters there. Most famous are the International Red Cross and Red Crescent Movement, the World Health Organization and the UN High Commissioner for Refugees.

One of the major tourist sights in the city is the Jet d'Eau, which has a special meaning for the people of Geneva. It is a symbol that, in the past, unlike many of the neighbouring areas, or cantons, Geneva did not try to conquer other lands. Instead the city turned its sights towards heaven – just like the Jet d'Eau!

The tallest fountain in the world is at Fountain Hills in Arizona, USA. When all three of its pumps are working, the water can reach a height of 190 m.

▲ The Jet d'Eau soars above the surface of Lake Geneva high into the sky.

Costa e Silva Bridge, Rio de Janeiro

The city of Rio de Janeiro, in Brazil, sprawls majestically around one side of Guanabara Bay, which sparkles a brilliant blue under the cloudless sky. Although not the capital, Rio bustles with activity as a major centre of commerce and a holiday attraction with its famous beaches, including Ipanema.

Guanabara Bay has been much admired for its beauty ever since it was discovered in 1502 by Portuguese explorers led by Amerigo Vespucci. While Rio lies on one side, the city of Niteroi stretches around the bay's opposite entrance. Linking the two cities is the amazingly long Costa e Silva Bridge, opened in 1972.

It stretches 13,900 m from one side of the bay to the other and linking assorted islands. It is a box girder bridge – the girders forming the bridge's top look like long boxes lying between the piers.

▲ The Costa e Silva bridge is nearly 14 km long half of which is over the sea across Guanabara Bay.

▼ It took five years to construct the bridge which joins Rio de Janeiro with Niteroi.

The longest bridging in the world is the Second Lake Pontchartrain Causeway in Louisiana, USA, completed in 1969. It is nearly 38.5 km long and links the towns of Mandeville and Metairie.

The Opera House, Sydney

Like huge sails billowing in the breeze, or pearly white shells floating on the water of Sydney Harbour, is how the Sydney Opera House appears. The shape of the building is actually based on segments of a sphere which had been pulled apart. It is one of the few modern buildings which most people can recognize from a photograph. To many it is almost a symbol of Australia itself.

The design was chosen in an international competition in the late 1950s. There were many people who objected to the building and many disputes arose during its construction. Finally, the Danish architect, Jørn Utzon, resigned leaving it half-built.

The building was eventually finished in 1973. As well as being an opera house, it also contains two theatres, a concert hall, restaurants, a cinema, art galleries and a library.

▼ Sydney Opera House stands on Bennelong Point, jutting out into the waters of Sydney Harbour.

▲ The whiteness of the building gleams in the sunlight. The building is made of concrete and the shine comes from the white tiles covering the outside.

The acoustics inside Sydney Opera House are not quite perfect. Jørn Utzon had designed the inside, too, but his plans were thrown out as it was thought he did not know enough about sound. However, his original plans show that the acoustics would have been perfect.

Sears Tower, Chicago

Chicago, Illinois, in the USA, can be called the home of the skyscraper. It was here in 1885 that the first building to use a frame to support its height, rather than the walls, was built. Today Chicago not only has some of the finest examples of skyscrapers from different ages, but also the world's tallest building – the Sears Tower. This sleek, dark building soars 443 m into the sky. It was built for Sears, Roebuck and Company, and completed in 1973.

Modern skyscrapers are made of a metal frame covered with glass. Because of their height, they are designed to withstand high winds gusting past the top floors. Sears Tower is made up of nine towers with their steel frames all welded together. This has also helped to reduce swaying in the wind, which is the result of the height of the building. The towers are all the same width, but are different heights. Black bands on the outside of the building cleverly hide the service areas.

▲ The building's bundle of nine towers and black bands around the outside give it a distinctive look.

The Sears Tower has 110 stories and is also the world's tallest office block. Some 16,500 people come to work here every day.
On the 103rd floor there is a viewing platform for visitors to look out on the city. It is 412 m above the ground and on a clear day four different US states can be seen.

▼ Sears Tower dominates the Chicago skyline.

Antarctic Base

Antarctica has always been a remote place – some people refer to it as the end of the earth. It is the coldest place on the planet and the ice is 3 km thick. Until humans arrived in the last few hundred years, only penguins lived there.

Many explorers died trekking across the white expanses of ice and snow in their bid to reach the South Pole. Now Antarctica is not so isolated, and scientists from different countries live there for up to a year at a time.

The scientists of the US Amundsen-Scott Station live here under a saucer-like dome 50 m across. Built in 1975, the aluminium metal shell houses a small village of buildings insulated against the cold. The living spaces are very small, because it is very expensive carrying building equipment to Antarctica.

▼ Living quarters inside the Antarctic base are cramped and space is limited.

▲ The Amundsen-Scott Station is drifting with the ice towards South America at the rate of 10 m a year.

Of the scientific stations on Antarctica, the US McMurdo Station has the largest community of scientists who stay for a year or longer. About 1,000 people live there in the summer, but fewer than 200 people stay for the winter.

Nuclear Plant, Kashwazaki-Kariwa

Since 1945, scientists have made electricity from nuclear energy. Exploding the nucleus of an atom creates large amounts of heat. This can be used to make steam to generate electricity – the most important peacetime use of nuclear energy. Over the years, Japan has tried to secure reliable energy supplies from other countries and at a reasonable price. It has also tried to produce as much power as possible – nuclear energy is one of those sources.

Since 1960, the Japanese government has agreed to the construction of forty new nuclear power plants. Only France produces more electricity from nuclear power. The biggest current Japanese reactor produces 8,814 megawatts of power. However, when No.6 and No.7 reactors of the Kashwazaki-Kariwa nuclear power station are finished, it will be Japan's largest nuclear site.

▲ Kashwazaki-Kariwa nuclear power station in Japan is now the world's largest nuclear site.

▼ The turbine (round section) and generator of one of the reactors at Kashwazaki-Kariwa. The engineer in the foreground gives an idea of its size.

Nuclear power uses less fuel than a coal- or oil-powered station, and it does not release dirty gases into the atmosphere. However, many people are worried about accepting nuclear power on a large scale, because of the potential dangers from radiation and because uranium remains radioactive for an extremely long time after it has been used.

Louisiana Superdome, New Orleans

The Louisiana Superdome is the largest indoor stadium in the world. It was built in 1975, and is a gigantic round structure in the centre of the city of New Orleans in Louisiana, USA. It is an impressive building – its massive windowless, curved walls towering up and curving outwards. The walls are crowned with the world's largest ever dome, which covers the stadium. The dome measures 210 m across and the stadium covers a total of 21 hectares!

The Superdome is the largest facility of its kind and can seat 76,791 people for a sports event, and even more for conventions. Underneath the dome, six enormous television screens give instant replays of events.

The Superdome is probably best known for the American football games played there, and it is home to the New Orleans Saints. Many college games are played there as well.

▶ The Louisiana Superdome is the largest covered stadium in the world.

▼ The high windowless walls of the Superdome tower above the ground and soar into the sky.

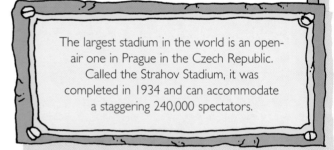

The largest stadium in the world is an open-air one in Prague in the Czech Republic. Called the Strahov Stadium, it was completed in 1934 and can accommodate a staggering 240,000 spectators.

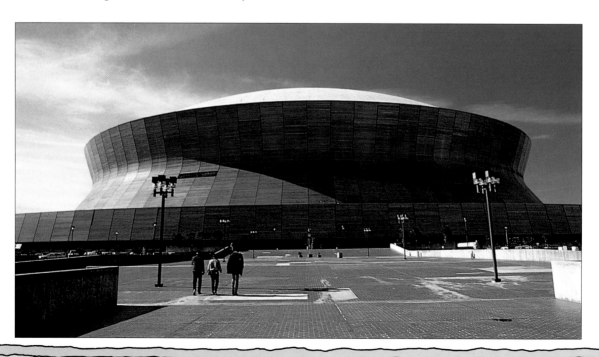

CN Tower, Toronto

Without a doubt, Toronto's most notable landmark is the Canadian National (CN) Tower. It rises above the skyline like a needle threaded with a bead. It stands near the harbour front of one of Canada's major cities, Toronto.

When it was completed in 1975, the CN Tower became the world's tallest structure at 553 m high. There have been other towers built which are taller, but they are held upright by supports or cables. The CN Tower has no supports – it is free-standing.

Although it is a communications tower, it has observation decks from which people can enjoy the view. Just over half way up the tower at 351 m is a restaurant, which turns slowly around. From here visitors can see the hills over 110 km away. Another viewing deck sits even further up the tower.

▼ The CN Tower rises above the skyscrapers of the Toronto skyline and it is reflected in the waters of Lake Toronto. On a clear day, visitors to the CN Tower's restaurant can see the hills 110 km away. Some people even say the mist rising from Niagara Falls is visible.

The record for the tallest tower was held by a radio mast at Konstantynow, north of Warsaw in Poland. The tower was 646 m tall, and was held upright with cables. But in 1991 it fell down. Now the tallest tower is a television transmitting tower in North Dakota, USA, built in 1963. It too is held up by supports and is 629 m high.

Inter-Provincial Pipeline

North America owns two of the world's longest pipelines. The Inter-Provincial Pipeline Company has a pipeline carrying crude oil across Canada and the USA. It starts in Edmonton, Canada and runs south for 2,856 km to Buffalo, in New York State, USA. It has a series of pumping stations along its length which maintain a flow of 31,367,145 litres of oil per day along the pipeline.

Pipelines are the most efficient way to transport oil. Crude oil is also transported by tankers, barges, trains and tanker trucks. Pipelines are expensive to build, but they are quite cheap to maintain and can be built in any terrain. The Trans-Alaska Pipeline runs 1,287 km from Prudhoe Bay inside the Arctic Circle to Valdez on Alaska's south coast, crossing three mountain ranges, more than 300 rivers and streams and nearly 640 kilometres of frozen land on the way. It was completed in 1977.

▼ Along the Inter-Provincial Pipeline there are several pumping stations such as this one near Edmonton.

The Inter-Provincial Pipeline is the longest crude oil pipeline in the world. However, the world's longest natural gas pipeline is the Trans-Canada Pipeline, which is said to be 9,099 km long.

Keck Telescope, Hawaii

The top of a volcano is an unlikely home for expensive technology, yet over a dozen telescopes sit on the top of Mauna Kea in Hawaii, USA. The telescopes look out unblinkingly at the sky, searching to unravel the mysteries of the universe and seek out life among the stars. The volcano makes a good setting to study the stars, as it is over 4,270 m high. One of the telescopes on the mountain top is the Keck Telescope, the world's largest optical telescope. The glass is 10 m across.

The Keck telescope is housed in a high, protective dome. Its huge mirror makes the Keck telescope very different to use, not just because of its size but because it is made up of thirty-six hexagonal mirrors about 1.8 m across. A computer lines up all the pieces to within 0.00003 mm twice a second, while a television monitor allows scientists to see what the telescope sees.

▲ The open dome of the Keck Telescope reveals its unique surface of thirty-six hexagonal mirrors. The dome protects the telescope's lenses.

The Keck Telescope began a new age in ground-based telescopes. It is twice the size of the Hale Telescope on Mount Palomar in California, USA, which for decades was the world's largest telescope. It was once thought impossible to build telescopes so large, but new technology has made it possible.

▼ The Keck Telescope (in the middle of the picture), stands on the summit of the dormant volcano Mauna Kea along with several other telescopes.

Open-cast Mine, Morewell

Morewell open-cast coal mine in the south of Australia is one of the largest manmade holes on Earth, so big that it would take at least two hours to walk around its edge. Open-cast mining is a way of extracting coal without having to tunnel underground. Explosives shatter the rock surrounding the coal, then giant power shovels and other earth-moving machines clear away the soil and rocks until the coal is reached.

Although an open-cast mine is impressive to look at, the damage it causes to the environment is horrifying. Nowadays, when mining has ended, some governments ask that all the land is returned as far as possible to the way it used to look. Soil is brought to fill the land, and grass and trees are planted.

▲ Thousands of tons of coal are removed from the mine each hour.

▼ Digging out coal by open-cast mining leaves large ugly holes in the ground. Now fortunately, when the mines are no longer used, most are filled and planted.

The deepest mine in the world is an underground gold mine in South Africa. It goes 3,581 m down into the ground. One of its shafts is 2,949 m deep, the longest in the world.

St Gottard Road Tunnel

The St Gottard Pass, through the Swiss Alps in southern Switzerland, has been an important route between northern Europe and Italy for hundreds of years. The mountain pass was known by the ancient Romans, but it was not used regularly until the fourteenth century. Today, a long winding motorway leads through the mountains to the mouth of the tunnel.

In 1882, a railway tunnel was opened through the mountains making travel easier. However, it was not until 1980 that the St Gottard Road Tunnel was opened. At present it is the longest road tunnel in the world and is 16 km in length. It was essential that the tunnel was built as the pass was closed every year in winter because of snow. The new tunnel, built 870 m up in the mountains, averages more than 1,500 vehicles passing through it per hour.

▲ The St Gottard Road Tunnel passes beneath the Alps and connects northern Europe with Italy.

At the time of the construction of the first St Gottard Tunnel, it was thought to be an outstanding technical achievement. However, nearly 200 men died during the building work, including the engineer in charge.

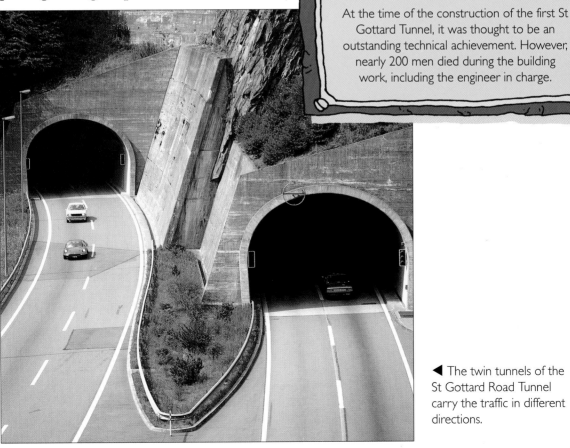

◀ The twin tunnels of the St Gottard Road Tunnel carry the traffic in different directions.

Humber Bridge, Humberside

The bridge with the longest span is so long that the towers at each end actually bend backwards by 36 mm to allow for the curve of the Earth's surface.

This bridge links two sides of the Humber River in northern England, 8 km upstream from the city of Hull. It took eight years to build and was finally opened in 1981 after much discussion among local people as to whether it should be built.

The Humber Bridge carries a four-lane road and pedestrian walkways. It was extremely expensive to build and was planned for an area which did not really have a traffic problem, but the town council of Hull decided to go ahead anyway. The result is the world's longest suspension bridge.

▲ The total length of the bridge is 2,220 m, although the main span is 1,410 m (between the towers).

▼ A spectacular view from one of the Humber Bridge's towers shows the long span of the bridge and just how much water in the river it covers.

When the Akaisho-Kaikyo road bridge in Japan is completed in 1998, it will have the longest span of any suspension bridge in the world. The main span will be 1,990 m and its towers will be the tallest bridge towers in existence, measuring 297 m, beating those of the Golden Gate Bridge in San Francisco (see page 71).

Itaipu Hydroelectric Power Plant

The Itaipu Dam changed the landscape of Brazil and Paraguay forever by covering miles of countryside and rainforest with water. The water is so deep that it even covers up a waterfall. The Paraná River was dammed to build the Itaipu Dam which lies between the two countries of Brazil and Paraguay. The two countries joined forces to build the dam, which cost US $20 billion.

Building went on from the mid-1970s to 1982. The Itaipu Dam rises sixty storeys high and the reservoir behind it stretches 161 km up river! It is the largest hydroelectric power plant in the world since being upgraded in 1990 to produce 12,600 megawatts from eighteen turbines. Its output of electricity is more than 20 per cent above that of its closest rival, Guri Dam in Venezuela.

▲ The Itaipu Dam in South America is the world's largest hydroelectric power plant.

The electricity produced by the Itaipu power plant is shared by Brazil and Paraguay. However, Paraguay only uses a tiny amount of the electricity, so it sells the majority of its share to Brazil.

▼ The enormous Itaipu Dam lies across the Paraná River which forms part of the border between the countries of Brazil and Paraguay.

Solar Furnace, Odeilo

Coal and oil are major sources of energy, but not very clean ones and possibly ones that are running out. The search is on to find clean ways of producing energy. The sun is a huge source of energy and, unlike coal or oil, is unlikely to run out. There are many ways of tapping the sun's energy, and people have already begun to do so by using solar panels, solar cells and large reflectors to produce electricity.

In the Pyrenees Mountains, at Odeilo in the south of France, a huge curved mirror is working to collect solar energy. It is the world's largest solar parabolic reflector. The enormous mirror focuses the sun's heat and light and can reach temperatures of 3,000°C. This heat is clean and completely free of dirty gases.

▲ At Odeilo, a series of sixty-three flat mirrors follow the path of the sun in the sky. The mirrors reflect the sun's rays on to the furnace mirror.

▼ The huge curved mirror at Odeilo, in the Pyrenees Mountains, collects the sun's rays. Solar power produces clean energy which lasts forever.

The heat from the mirror can be concentrated on to a boiler to produce steam for a heating system in a building, or for driving a type of motor, or turbine, to produce electricity.

The largest-ever solar power plant is in the Mojave Desert in California, USA. It was operated by one company until it ran out of money and the site is now owned by three companies. The installation has 650,000 computer-controlled parabolic mirrors which track the sun across the sky.

Thames Barrier, London

The massive gleaming fins of the Thames Barrier rise out of the water looking as if they belong to a long sea monster. The barrier was built between 1972 and 1984 to give London protection against floods and high tides in the River Thames.

The barrier lies 13 km down river from central London, at Woolwich. The barrier stretches 521 m across the river. Ten enormous moveable steel gates weighing from 406 to 3,760 tonnes are linked by the steel covered concrete piers. The gates will hold back the weight of millions of tonnes of water when they are raised.

The gates are rounded at the bottom, like quarter-moon shapes. Usually, they pivot to lie flat on the bed of the river, allowing boats to pass between the piers. If there is any danger of flooding, the gates, which are 18 m high, are raised by massive rocker beams.

The last major high tide along the Thames was in 1953. London itself was saved the worst of the flooding, but further down river sea walls failed and 300 people died.

▲ The gates of the Thames Barrier usually lie on the river-bed, allowing the normal traffic of boats on the river to pass between the piers.

▼ When the level of the River Thames rises, due to heavy rain and high tides, the gates of the barrier are raised.

Mir Space Station

We are probably all fairly used to the idea of humans travelling into space and returning again, but we forget that some people live in space for months at a time. Space stations like the Russian *Mir* station may fly over our heads many times during a month – they are several miles high and we cannot see them.

The *Mir*, which means 'peace' in Russian, was first launched into space in 1986. Two months later, two Russian cosmonauts were sent up to become the first occupants of the station. *Mir* had six docking ports for extra modules or other spacecraft, and a year after its launch the first of the extra modules was sent up to be locked on to the space

station. These interlocking modules have been launched into space with other Russian space craft.

Other modules have been added to enlarge the station, giving more living space and extra working room. One of the modules has allowed *Mir* to become a space factory. Materials can be made which require the unique environment of space and which cannot be made on Earth. Recently the US space shuttles have linked up with *Mir* on two occasions and delivered supplies of food.

▼ *Mir* is made of interlocking modules which are launched into space. One of the modules can provide a laboratory for work on astrophysics. Another module has an airlock so that the cosmonauts can perform space walks and carry out maintenance on the outside of the station.

Many of *Mir*'s cosmonauts have broken records for the length of time they have spent in space. The most recent record was broken at the beginning of 1995 when Dr Valeriy Poilakov spent 430 days in space.

Oosterscheldedam, Netherlands

On 1 February 1953, the North Sea washed over dykes to flood much of the southern Netherlands. The Dutch government immediately decided something must be done to protect this area from another catastrophic flood and launched the Delta Project. The project aimed to mend and strengthen dykes, build several small dams and a large one across a major river mouth, the Oosterschelde, where three rivers meet.

Many people complained that a large dam would destroy wildlife in the area and end many fishermen's jobs. So the government built a storm surge barrier instead. It is like a dam, but with a series of huge gates letting water in and out. These close if there is a danger of storms

▲ The Oosterscheldedam has sixty-five concrete piers, sixty-two steel gates and stretches 9 km across the mouth of the Oosterschelde river.

or flooding, saving the land behind. The storm barrier was opened in October 1986 – the longest tidal river barrage in the world.

▼ The gates of the storm surge barrier need to be raised when high tides occur, perhaps once a year.

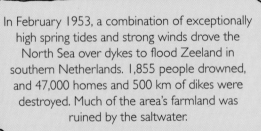

In February 1953, a combination of exceptionally high spring tides and strong winds drove the North Sea over dykes to flood Zeeland in southern Netherlands. 1,855 people drowned, and 47,000 homes and 500 km of dikes were destroyed. Much of the area's farmland was ruined by the saltwater.

Wind Farm, Altamont Pass

The earliest windmills known were built in Iran in about the seventh century AD. The oldest Dutch windmill only dates from around 1450. Modern windmills, used to generate electricity, are called wind turbines and do not look much like the traditional windmill! They have 2–3 blades like a propellor and a tail vane to keep them pointing at the wind.

Because one turbine does not produce much electricity, a number of turbines are placed together in a large area to produce a 'wind farm'. Over 90 per cent of wind-generated electricity comes from California, USA, mostly from wind farms in mountain passes.

The world's largest wind farm is at Altamont Pass, east of San Francisco in California, where over 7,000 wind turbines sit in a 207.2 sq. km area. The farm produces a million megawatt hours of power a year – enough to satisfy a city as big as San Francisco.

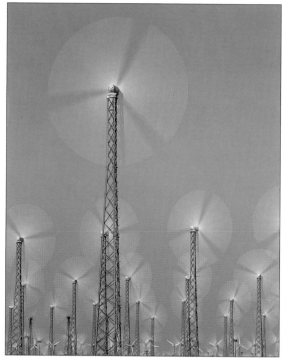

▲ The most popular type of wind turbine has two or three blades, which are like propellors. Each one can generate more then 2 megawatts of electricity in a moderate wind.

The largest wind turbine in the world is the GEC MOD–5a installation on the north shore of Oahu in the Hawaiian Islands of the Pacific. It has blades that are 122 m long and produces 7.3 megawatts of power when the wind reaches a speed of 51.5 kph.

◀ The world's largest wind farm at Altamont Pass in California has over 7,000 wind turbines. Not many places have reliable winds that blow constantly. That is why wind farms are generally located on mountains or coasts.

CERN Particle Accelerator

Deep under the neat, green countryside close to the Swiss–French border lies a maze of tunnels, covering 556 hectares and used for experiments on atoms. This is the home of an international scientific body, the European Organization for Nuclear Research (CERN).

CERN has the most powerful facilities in the world to test nuclear particles. The heat that these experiments produce can be hotter than the centre of the sun. Although scientists here are exploring the tiniest particles in the universe, smaller than atoms, the largest machines on Earth are needed.

CERN's particle accelerator, which gives out the fierce heat, is more than 6.5 km long and one of the largest machines ever built. The ring-shaped accelerator is fifteen storeys underground and made of concrete, built in 1976. CERN also has an even bigger tunnel which was built in 1989. It is 27 km in diameter.

▶ The CERN site seen from the air shows the size of the loops where particles are tested.

▼ The experiments with colliding particles are undertaken in tunnels deep underground.

Other particle accelerators are different, although they have only two shapes, round or straight. We all have a primitive form of a particle accelerator at home – the television. Inside its tube electricity heats a metal filament. Negatively charged electrons are accelerated through a positively charged grid. A magnet steers them at the screen which glows with the collisions.

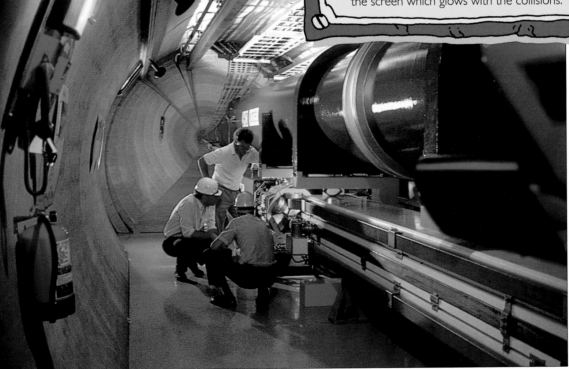

Edwin P. Hubble Space Telescope

Although there are large telescopes on earth looking at distant worlds, a space telescope can provide an even better image of the stars and galaxies. The earth's atmosphere blocks or bends light from stars and galaxies, blurring the images a telescope receives. A telescope above the earth's atmosphere can capture detail impossible to obtain from earth.

The Hubble Space Telescope is a huge reflecting telescope which orbits 580 km above the earth's surface. The telescope weighs an incredible 11 tonnes, and its mirror is 240 cm across. It was launched into space on a US space shuttle by NASA in April 1990.

The telescope is controlled by radio commands from the Goddard Space Flight Center in Maryland, USA. So far, it has produced some remarkable pictures by transmitting radio waves to astronomers on the ground.

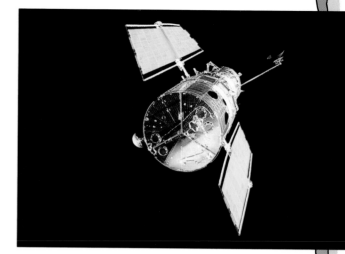

▲ The Hubble Telescope orbits high above the earth's atmosphere, and gets a clear view of the universe.

Two months after the Hubble Telescope was first launched in space, scientists discovered that it was producing blurred images – one of the mirrors inside the telescope was made to the wrong specifications. This was corrected in 1994 by space shuttle astronauts.

◄ The Hubble Telescope is berthed on the space shuttle *Endeavor*'s cargo bay in preparation for astronauts to carry out servicing tasks on the telescope.

Troll Platform

The mammoth *Troll* platform forms part of Europe's largest gas project. It will provide 10 per cent of Europe's gas needs well into the twenty-first century as it pumps gas from the sea-bed. It is not just the tallest platform, at 472 m, to stand on the sea-bottom, but also one of the largest manmade objects ever made and the tallest concrete structure, too.

The platform's legs, which give it such a height, are made of concrete and steel and are 369 m tall. It took ten tug boats four days to pull the platform from Stavanger on the coast of Norway to its resting place in the North Sea. One of the *Troll*'s features is that it has been made by the Shell Company to last for a long time – well over fifty years.

▶ The *Troll* platform has legs which are made of concrete and steel. There is enough steel in them to make fifteen Eiffel Towers. Most of the legs will remain underwater because the platform is designed to withstand extremely strong winds.

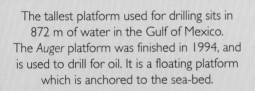

The tallest platform used for drilling sits in 872 m of water in the Gulf of Mexico. The *Auger* platform was finished in 1994, and is used to drill for oil. It is a floating platform which is anchored to the sea-bed.

▼ The *Troll* platform took four days to be pulled out to sea by tug boats from the Norwegian coast to the North Sea.

Pepsi-Max, The Big One, Blackpool

A light meal is advisable before taking a ride on the Pepsi-Max, The Big One, on Blackpool Pleasure Beach. It is the world's tallest and fastest roller-coaster, hurtling along at speeds which can be as high as 128 kph. Blackpool, in north-western England, is a traditional British seaside resort, where there is still plenty to do for holiday makers – going to funfairs, visiting the three piers, enjoying rides on trams and viewing the night-time illuminations from the top of the tower, for example.

Pepsi-Max, The Big One, cost £12 million to build and was opened in 1994. The steel monster takes courageous passengers round a mile-long journey of stomach-churning, white-knuckled fear. The first drop of the roller-coaster falls 64 m straight down!

▲ Frightened and excited passengers begin hurtling down the first and highest drop of the Pepsi-Max, The Big One, in Blackpool.

▼ As a train begins the first drop you can see just how steep and tall the roller-coaster actually is.

Two roller-coasters in the USA share the highest vertical drop of 68.5 m.
One is the Steel Phantom in Pennsylvania; the other is the Desperado in Nevada.
The roller-coaster with the highest loop, which is 43 m above the ground, is the Viper in California, USA.

Channel Tunnel, Britain/France

For centuries people talked about building a tunnel under the English Channel – the narrow stretch of sea that separates France and England. In 1994, this became reality with the opening of the Channel Tunnel. Now passengers can ride a train from London to Paris and arrive in just a few hours.

The Channel Tunnel is 48 km long. About 35 km are underwater, making it the longest underwater tunnel in the world. There are actually three tunnels – two for trains and a smaller service tunnel between them. The tunnel was cut in about forty-two months, although building lasted from 1987 to 1994.

Eleven boring machines dug nonstop through 4.6 m of rock an hour on the three tunnels. Digging was carried out from both ends, and to ensure that the tunnels met in the middle, the digging machines were computer controlled.

▲ Here construction workers progress with the laying of the rails inside the tunnels before the project was finished in 1994. Each tunnel works in a single direction only, with passenger terminals at each end of the tunnel.

The world's longest tunnel is the Seikan Tunnel in Japan. It links the two islands of Honshu and Hokkaido. It was completed in 1988 and it is 53 km long. However, only 22.5 km are underwater.

▼ Trains travelling through the tunnel carry cars stacked on double-decker carriages, as well as trucks, coaches and foot passengers in carriages.

Kansai Airport, Osaka

Japan's newest international airport sits like a long steel insect resting on a manmade island 5 km out to sea. Opened in 1994, Kansai International Airport lies in the Bay of Osaka. It was built there because Osaka wanted an airport within thirty minutes of the city centre, and this was the only direction possible.

The airport took only six years to complete, but before that the island had to be built. It consists of crushed rock 20 m deep, which rests on soft clay. The island is joined to the mainland by a long bridge, which carries road and rail passengers directly to the airport terminal.

The sleek glass and steel building is shaped like a gleaming aeroplane wing. Although there is only one runway, there is room for forty-one aeroplanes to use the airport at one time. In the next few years, over 100,000 people are expected to pass through the airport each day.

The changes in the clay and rock of the island are monitored by a computer, which keeps tabs on every aspect of the airport's services and structure. It controls the pumping of cool air into the building for most of every day.

▼ Kansai International Airport lies on an artificial island in the sea. The building is supported by hundreds of steel columns sunk into a raft of concrete, which is jacked up or down as the island shifts in position.

Pont de Normandie

As it stands guard over the mud flats of the river Seine in northern France, the Pont de Normandie looks like a huge spider's web of steel cables stretched over concrete towers. It is a new bridge which opened in January 1995 linking two towns, Honfleur and Le Havre. The Pont de Normandie is a cable-stayed bridge. This sort of bridge is similar to a suspension bridge like the Golden Gate Bridge (see page 71), but the cables which hold it up are linked directly from the towers to the bridge.

The bridge was built in thirty-three sections. The central section was the last piece to be slotted into place – this was done by lifting it from below. The weight of the bridge is carried by 2,000 km of cable. The twin concrete towers are 215 m high, and stand in foundations which are as deep as a twenty-storey building. The central span of the Pont de Normandie is 856 m, but this does not include the approaches to the bridge. Altogether the bridge is 2,200 m in length.

◀ The Pont de Normandie while still under construction. The roadway is still being built and the towers are not yet complete.

▼ The Pont de Normandie has been planned to save motorists time in their journeys across northern France. It is estimated that 6,000 vehicles already drive over the bridge each day.

A hundred years ago, the French painter, Claude Monet, painted the spot where the Pont de Normandie stands. Not only did it make the scene famous, but Monet created a scandal by using a brand-new style of painting called Impressionism. Now the scene has been changed forever by the new bridge.

[ ] – See page in text

A _____	He ordered a lighthouse to be built [8]
B ____	(1) Bishop of Caesarea, who urged people to settle in Cappadocia [39]; (2) Russian saint, the 'holy fool', buried in Moscow [49]
C _____	Founder of a corporation that made cars; a New York skyscraper bears his name [69]
D _ _____	Head of construction of the Suez Canal and planner of the Panama Canal [59]
E _____	Designer of a famous tower in Paris [62] and of the Statue of Liberty [61]
F _____	Designer of the geodesic dome [81]
G _____	Name of St George in Ethiopia [43]
H _____	A space telescope is named for him [102]
I _____	First name of the inventor and designer whose works include the Suspension Bridge over the Avon Gorge, England [57]
J _____	Emperor who built Hagia Sophia, Istanbul [29]
K _____	One of the royal builders of the pyramids of Giza, Egypt [11]
L ____ ___	King of France who built Versailles [54]
M _____	Ruler of Caria who built a huge tomb at Halicarnassus [8]
N _____	Roman god to whom temple in Paestum, Italy, was dedicated [20]
O _____ _____	The New O_____ S_____ football team are based in the Superdrome, Louisiana [88]
P _____	He carved the statue of Zeus at Olympia – one of the seven wonders of the world [9]
Q ____ _____	Wife of Prince Albert, organizer of the 1851 London exhibition for which Crystal Palace was built [58]
R _____	One of the US presidents whose face is carved in the side of Mt Rushmore, South Dakota [72]
S __ _____	The First Emperor of China who planned the Great Wall [23]
T _____	Legendary Greek prince who killed the Minotaur in Knossos, Crete [14]
U ____	Danish architect, designer of the Sydney Opera House [84]
V _____	First name of the Russian cosmonaut who has spent longest in space [98]
W _____	Composer on whose opera settings Neuschwanstein Castle was based [60]
_____X	Legendary guardian of the pyramids [11]
Y ____	Tents used by the Mongols on the plains of Siberia [37]
Z ____	The Step Pyramid was built in Egypt for him [10]

A ____	High Dam built in the late 1970s in Egypt [15]
B _____	Site of the Hanging Gardens [9] and of the Ishtar Gate [17]
C ____	Country at southern end of the Pan-American Highway [75]
D _____	This dam provides most of the electricity for the mines along the Dneiper River [78]
E _____	Buddhists, Hindus and Jains all carved temples at this site in India [33]
F _____	The Vehicle Assembly Building, where rockets and space shuttles are made, is in this state of the USA [79]
G ____ ____	Lake formed by damming the Chagras River while constructing the Panama Canal [66]
H _____ _____	The longest suspension bridge in the world in 1996 [94]
I _____	Site of hydroelectric power plant on the Brazil/Paraguay border [95]
J _____	The rose-red city of Petra is in this country of the Middle East [26]
K _ _____	Japan's newest airport, on a manmade island off Osaka [106]
L _____	12th century churches cut from rock are at this site in Ethiopia [43]
M ___ _____	Site of cliff dwellings in Colorado, USA [41]
N ____	The Romans built the Pont du Gard here [25]
O ___	The Great Serpent Mound is in this state of the USA [19]
P _____	The largest temple on the Acropolis, Athens [21]
Q _____	This is what the Colosseum in Rome was used for after the 5th century [24]
R ____	Name of river in France and huge barrage built across it for a tidal power station [80]
S ____ ____	Golden-spired pagoda in Yangon, Myanmar [46]
_	Home of the Temple of the Giant Jaguar [32]
T ____	Ancient city in Mesopotamia, site of the Great Ziggurat [12]
U _	
V _____	City in Italy lying in a lagoon and crisscrossed by canals [48]
W _____	State of the USA where the Columbia River is held back by the Grand Coulee Dam [73]
___X_____	Home of a world-famous lighthouse [8]
Y _____	The Hall of Dreams at the temple of Horyuji, Nara, Japan [30]
	Stone city and country in Africa [44]

Answers can be found on page 111

Index

Picture Acknowledgements

t = top, b = bottom

A/S Norske Shell: 7 & 103t, 103b.
Audience Planners: USTS, 41t; USTTA, cover & 72b.
Australian Tourist Commission: 84t, cover & 84b.
Bildaghentur Schuster: 76t.
Blackpool Pleasure Beach: cover & 104t, 104b.
CCIH: C. Louvet, 107b.
CERN Photo: 101t, 101b.
Corbis-Bettmann/UPI: 8b, 17b, 72t, 73b, 36b, cover & 61t, 74.
D.G. Davaris, Athens: 18b.
Directoraat-Gerneral Rijswaterstaat: 70t, 70b, 99t, 99b. Tom Owen Edmunds: 50t. Fiat SpA: 67t, 67b.
Francesco Venturi: 30t.

Generation Victoria: Jenny Richie 92t, 92b.
Hulton Deutsch Collection: 57t, 57b, 58t, 58b, 63t, 78t, 83t, 83b, 93t, cover & 105b.
The Image Bank: 45t, Alex Barkoff, Stockphotos 88b; Luis Castaneda 88t; Grant Faint 54b; Peter Frey cover & 95b; Jorge's Estudio 95t; Gerhard Oscheidle 31t; Marc Romanelli 48b; Guido Alberto Rossi 48t, cover, 6 & 81; Haraald Sund cover & 50b. I.P.L. Inc.: 90t, 90b.
James Harpur: 10b, 11t, 20t, 20b, 22t, 22b, 29t. Japan National Tourist Office: 106. Roger Kohn: 14b, 42b, 65b, 42t. Magnum Photos: Jean Gaumy 107t. The Mansell Collection: 8t, 9t, 23b, cover & 24t, 28b, 40b, 51b, cover & 55t, 59t, 62t, 66b, 68b. NASA: cover & 79, cover & 102t, 102b. Ohio Historical Society: 19b.

OSF: Ronald Toms 80t, 80b.
Photo Tenis: 18t, 10t.
Robert Harding Picture Library: 12t, 12b, 14t, 15t, 17t, 19t, 1 & 23t, 24b, 26b, 27t, 27b, 31b, cover & 32t, 32b, 34b, 35b, 37t, 40t, 43t, 43b, 44t, 44b, 46b, 47t, 6 & 47b, cover & 49t, 49b, 52t, 54t, 55b, 60t, 60b, 66t, 69b, 73t, 76b, 85b, 86t, 86b, cover & 94b; C. Bowman cover & 25t, 53;, Jeremy Bright 38b; Jackum Brown cover & 34t; Philip Craven cover & 15b; Diethelm, Bildagentur Schuster 93b; Nigel Francis cover & 62b, 69t; Robert Francis 94t; Robert Frerck 77; Grossmann, Imagine Explorer 105t; Ian Griffiths 51t; Simon Harris 61b; Gavin Heller 41b; F. Jack Jackson 59b; Michael Jenner 82; Layda, Bildagentur Schuster 45b; David Lomax 78b; C. Martin 89t; Photri 37b; Roy

Rainford 21t; Walter Rawlings cover & 11b, 71; Rolf Richardson 26t; Christopher Rennie 21, 35t; Bill Ross Westlight, 75t; Scholz, Bildagentur Schuster 30b; Israel Talby cover & 64; Paul van Riel 28t; Weisker, Bildagentur Schuster 36t; JHC Wilson 46t; Adam Woolfitt 16t, 6 & 16b, 25b, 33t, 33b, 38t, cover, 7 & 52b, 68t, 96t, 96b, 97t.
Russia & Republics Photolibrary: 56t, 56b.
Science Photo Library: Lowell Georgia 100b; John Mead 100t; Novosti Press Agency 98; Roger Ressmeyer 91t; Royal Observatory 91b.
South American Pictures: 75b. Tigerhill Studio: 85t.
Tokyo Electric Company: 87t, 87b. Turkey National Tourist Office: 29b.
Zooid Pictures: 13t, 13b, 39t, 39b, 63b, 65t, 97b